THIS BOOK BELONGS TO

_____

_____

START DATE _____ / _____ / _____

HE READS TRUTH

EXECUTIVE

**FOUNDER /
CHIEF EXECUTIVE OFFICER**
Raechel Myers

**CO-FOUNDER /
CHIEF CONTENT OFFICER**
Amanda Bible Williams

CHIEF OPERATING OFFICER
Ryan Myers

EXECUTIVE ASSISTANT
Sarah Andereck

EDITORIAL

EDITORIAL DIRECTOR
Jessica Lamb

CONTENT EDITOR
Kara Gause

ASSOCIATE EDITORS
Bailey Gillespie
Ellen Taylor
Tameshia Williams

EDITORIAL ASSISTANT
Hannah Little

CREATIVE

CREATIVE DIRECTOR
Jeremy Mitchell

LEAD DESIGNER
Kelsea Allen

DESIGNERS
Abbey Benson
Davis DeLisi
Annie Glover

MARKETING

MARKETING DIRECTOR
Krista Juline Williams

MARKETING MANAGER
Katie Matuska Pierce

SOCIAL MEDIA MANAGER
Ansley Rushing

COMMUNITY SUPPORT SPECIALIST
Margot Williams

SHIPPING & LOGISTICS

LOGISTICS MANAGER
Lauren Gloyne

SHIPPING MANAGER
Sydney Bess

CUSTOMER SUPPORT SPECIALIST
Katy McKnight

FULFILLMENT SPECIALISTS
Abigail Achord
Cait Baggerman
Kamiren Passavanti

SUBSCRIPTION INQUIRIES
orders@hereadstruth.com

CONTRIBUTORS

ARTWORK
Jaye Whitehead (18, 20, 36, 52, 54, 62, 84, 110, 122, 148, 152)

PHOTOGRAPHY
Michael Stricklin (86)

RECIPE
Taylor and Everly Lamb (138)

SPECIAL THANKS
John Greco, MDiv

COLOPHON

This book was printed offset in Nashville, Tennessee, on 60# Lynx Opaque Text under the direction of He Reads Truth. The cover is 100# matte with a soft touch aqueous coating and Infinity Foil 88.

COPYRIGHT

HEREADSTRUTH.COM

@HEREADSTRUTH

Download the He Reads Truth app, available for iOS and Android.

ADVENT 2020

JESUS CHRIST IS BORN

Advent is a time to prepare Him room and to orient our hearts, homes, and minds to the ungraspable magnitude and true meaning of Christmas.

Advent is a season of remembrance, of preparing our hearts to celebrate the birth of Jesus. There is a roundedness, a fullness, to the incarnation that, when we engage with Advent as a season, is not lost on us come Christmas morning. If we only open our Bibles to Luke 2 on December 25th, we can certainly celebrate the miraculous birth of our Savior. But when we open our Bibles on December 1st—and again on the 2nd and 3rd, and every day of the Advent season—we have the opportunity to experience a fuller picture of *why* Jesus came and *what* He came to do.

When we slow down and consider all the incarnation of God accomplishes, we understand that the birth of Jesus truly is worth shouting from the rooftops! Remembering and celebrating the arrival of the One who came to bless the nations, to fulfill the Law, to be the actual Lamb of God cannot be accomplished in a single cantata or even a Christmas Eve service. It merits an entire season.

This is why we, along with Christians around the globe and across the centuries, observe the Advent season. It is a time to prepare Him room and to orient our hearts, homes, and minds to the ungraspable magnitude of the true meaning of Christmas. It takes time.

We look forward to reading the whole-Scripture story of Christmas directly from God's Word with you. You'll notice that each day's reading answers an aspect of this question: "Why did Jesus come?"

If you have celebrated Advent with us before, you may remember our nine-years-running tradition of choosing a Christmas carol lyric for our book title. This year, our title comes from "Go, Tell It on the Mountain." This familiar spiritual captures the jubilant nature of Christmas—no matter our circumstances, no matter what is happening in our lives and in our world, the news that "Jesus Christ is born" is something to proclaim and celebrate.

Our hope is that, as individuals and a community, we will consecrate Advent 2020 as a season of remembering not only *that* Jesus came, but *why* He came. Even more, as we grow in understanding of the truly good news of Christ's offering, let's be a people who can't keep it to ourselves! Let's invite others in and celebrate together the miracle of Jesus's birth and our rebirth. Let's Go! Tell it on the mountain: the news that surpasses, informs, and redeems all other news. Jesus Christ is born!

Merry Christmas,

THE HE READS TRUTH TEAM

Each He Reads Truth resource is thoughtfully and artfully designed to highlight the beauty, goodness, and truth of Scripture in a way that reflects the themes of each curated reading plan.

For our Advent 2020 Legacy Book, we incorporated watercolor textures from Jaye Bird, our featured artist for this plan. These textures—and the featured photography—offer a contemporary take on an ancient celebration.

ABCDEFGHIJKLM
NOPQRSTUVWXY

abcdefghijklmnopqrstuvwx

Each book in the He Reads Truth Legacy Series™ provides space to read and study Scripture, make notes, and record prayers. As you build your library, you will have a record of your Bible-reading journey to reference and pass down.

SCRIPTURE READING

Designed to begin on November 29 (the first Sunday of Advent), this Legacy Book presents daily readings for the 2020 Advent season.

RESPONSE

Each daily reading features a prayer prompt and question for reflection.

GRACE DAY

Use Saturdays to catch up on your reading, pray, and reflect on the advent of Christ.

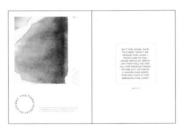

SUNDAYS OF ADVENT

Each Sunday features a short Scripture passage and reflection for the four Sundays of Advent and the first Sunday of Christmastide.

EXTRAS

This book features additional tools to help you gain a deeper understanding of the text.

Devotionals corresponding to each
daily reading can be found in the
Advent 2020: Jesus Christ Is Born
reading plan at HeReadsTruth.com or
on the He Reads Truth app.

Advent 2020: Jesus Christ Is Born

PLAN OVERVIEW   4 Weeks

"Go, tell it on the mountain that Jesus Christ
is born!" Two thousand years ago, the birth of
a baby boy fulfilled God's earliest promises
and answered generations of heartache.
Jesus was born to bring light to a world in
darkness, to seek and save the lost, to heal
our wounds with His, and to make all things
new. This four-week Advent experience
features daily Scripture reading carefully
curated for the Advent season. Join us as we
anticipate and remember the profound
miracle that Jesus Christ Is Born.

Day 1   **The First Sunday of Advent**

TABLE OF CONTENTS

Why was Jesus born? What did He come to do? Each day in this reading plan offers one answer to these questions.

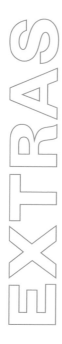

DECEMBER

SUNDAY	MONDAY	TUESDAY	WEDNESDAY
NOV 29 **ADVENT BEGINS**	30	DEC 1	2
6 **SECOND SUNDAY OF ADVENT**	7	8	9 Today is the last day to order from HeReadsTruth.com for delivery in time for Christmas!
13 **THIRD SUNDAY OF ADVENT**	14	15	16
20 **FOURTH SUNDAY OF ADVENT**	21	22 **CINNAMON ROLLS** Pick up the ingredients to make Christmas morning cinnamon rolls.	23
27 **FIRST SUNDAY OF CHRISTMASTIDE**	28 **FOR THE RECORD** Turn to page 154 to reflect on 2020 and pray for the year ahead.	29	30

THURSDAY	FRIDAY	SATURDAY	NOTES
3	4	5	
10	11	12	
17	18	19	
24 CHRISTMAS EVE	25	26 CHRISTMASTIDE BEGINS	
31 NEW YEAR'S EVE			

Scan this QR code to listen to our Advent playlist on Spotify.

DECK THE HALLS
Gather the supplies you need for making garlands.

CHRISTMAS DAY

I WILL HONOUR CHRISTMAS IN MY HEART, AND TRY TO KEEP IT ALL THE YEAR.
CHARLES DICKENS

WHAT IS ADVENT?

ADVENT
COMES FROM A LATIN WORD MEANING "COMING" OR "ARRIVAL."

The season of Advent has always been one of hope and expectation. From the first Sunday of Advent until Christmas Eve, we await the celebration of Jesus's birth. But this season of anticipation doesn't end on Christmas Day.

As followers of Christ, we are a people living between two advents: the coming of Jesus as a baby in Bethlehem and His future triumphant return as the King of kings (Lk 2:11-15; Rv 21:5-7). Since the fourth century, believers across the globe have observed Advent to remember Jesus's birth and anticipate His return.

A SEASON TO REMEMBER

THE FIRST ADVENT

During Advent, we remember that Jesus came as the fulfillment of Old Testament promises, the answer to the prayers of generations who anticipated the promised Messiah. We celebrate not only His birth, but also the life He was born to live.

A SEASON TO ANTICIPATE

THE SECOND ADVENT

We also anticipate Jesus's promised return, when He will one day come again, bringing with Him the fullness of His kingdom. On that future day, every tear will be wiped away; there will be no more pain, grief, or death. All things will be made new, all that is wrong will be made right, and the eternal dwelling place of God will be with His people.

Then I heard a loud voice from the throne: Look, God's dwelling is with humanity, and he will live with them. They will be his peoples, and God himself will be with them and will be their God. He will wipe away every tear from their eyes. Death will be no more; grief, crying, and pain will be no more, because the previous things have passed away.

Then the one seated on the throne said, "Look, I am making everything new." He also said, "Write, because these words are faithful and true." Then he said to me, "It is done! I am the Alpha and the Omega, the beginning and the end. I will freely give to the thirsty from the spring of the water of life."

REVELATION 21:3–6

THIS ADVENT SEASON, WE WILL REMEMBER WHY JESUS CAME AND WHAT HE CAME TO DO—AND WE'LL CELEBRATE JESUS AS THE LIVING SAVIOR AND FOREVER KING WHO HAS PROMISED TO COME AGAIN.

THIS IS THE HEART OF ADVENT.

HOPE

THE FIRST SUNDAY OF ADVENT

On this first Sunday of Advent, we celebrate the hope we have in Christ. Spend this week memorizing or meditating on Micah 7:7, thanking God for the hope of our salvation.

This Advent season, we will spend the Sundays leading up to Christmas reflecting on the themes of the four candles lit in traditional Advent services: hope, peace, joy, and love. Advent is a season of joyful anticipation, and these passages remind us of the comfort and delight we find in Immanuel, God with us.

> # BUT I WILL LOOK TO THE LORD; I WILL WAIT FOR THE GOD OF MY SALVATION. MY GOD WILL HEAR ME.

MICAH 7:7

JESUS CHRIST

IS

BORN...

03

To Show Us Perfect Love

To Heal Our Wounds

To Be the Lamb of God

To Be the Firstfruits of the Resurrection

To Make All Things New

04

To Be God with Us

To Bring Mercy

To Exalt the Humble

To Offer Us His Peace

DAY 02

TO BRING LIGHT TO A WORLD IN DARKNESS

BIRTH OF THE PRINCE OF PEACE

¹ Nevertheless, the gloom of the distressed land will not be like that of the former times when he humbled the land of Zebulun and the land of Naphtali. But in the future he will bring honor to the way of the sea, to the land east of the Jordan, and to Galilee of the nations.

² The people walking in darkness
have seen a great light;
a light has dawned
on those living in the land of darkness.
³ You have enlarged the nation
and increased its joy.
The people have rejoiced before you
as they rejoice at harvest time
and as they rejoice when dividing spoils.
⁴ For you have shattered their oppressive yoke
and the rod on their shoulders,
the staff of their oppressor,
just as you did on the day of Midian.
⁵ For every trampling boot of battle
and the bloodied garments of war
will be burned as fuel for the fire.
⁶ For a child will be born for us,
a son will be given to us,
and the government will be on his shoulders.
He will be named
Wonderful Counselor, Mighty God,
Eternal Father, Prince of Peace.
⁷ The dominion will be vast,
and its prosperity will never end.
He will reign on the throne of David
and over his kingdom,
to establish and sustain it
with justice and righteousness from now on and forever.
The zeal of the Lord of Armies will accomplish this.

ISAIAH 60:1–3, 19–22

THE LORD'S GLORY IN ZION

[1] Arise, shine, for your light has come,
and the glory of the LORD shines over you.
[2] For look, darkness will cover the earth,
and total darkness the peoples;
but the LORD will shine over you,
and his glory will appear over you.
[3] Nations will come to your light,
and kings to your shining brightness.

…

[19] The sun will no longer be your light by day,
and the brightness of the moon will not shine on you.
The LORD will be your everlasting light,
and your God will be your splendor.
[20] Your sun will no longer set,
and your moon will not fade;
for the LORD will be your everlasting light,
and the days of your sorrow will be over.
[21] All your people will be righteous;
they will possess the land forever;
they are the branch I planted,
the work of my hands,
so that I may be glorified.
[22] The least will become a thousand,
the smallest a mighty nation.
I am the LORD;
I will accomplish it quickly in its time.

¹ In the beginning was the Word, and the Word was with God, and the Word was God. ² He was with God in the beginning. ³ All things were created through him, and apart from him not one thing was created that has been created. ⁴ In him was life, and that life was the light of men. ⁵ That light shines in the darkness, and yet the darkness did not overcome it.

⁶ There was a man sent from God whose name was John. ⁷ He came as a witness to testify about the light, so that all might believe through him. ⁸ He was not the light, but he came to testify about the light. ⁹ The true light that gives light to everyone was coming into the world.

2 CORINTHIANS 4:6

For God who said, "Let light shine out of darkness," has shone in our hearts to give the light of the knowledge of God's glory in the face of Jesus Christ.

EPHESIANS 5:8–14

⁸ For you were once darkness, but now you are light in the Lord. Walk as children of light— ⁹ for the fruit of the light consists of all goodness, righteousness, and truth— ¹⁰ testing what is pleasing to the Lord. ¹¹ Don't participate in the fruitless works of darkness, but instead expose them. ¹² For it is shameful even to mention what is done by them in secret. ¹³ Everything exposed by the light is made visible, ¹⁴ for what makes everything visible is light. Therefore it is said:

> Get up, sleeper, and rise up from the dead,
> and Christ will shine on you.

REVELATION 21:23-27

[23] The city does not need the sun or the moon to shine on it, because the glory of God illuminates it, and its lamp is the Lamb. [24] The nations will walk by its light, and the kings of the earth will bring their glory into it. [25] Its gates will never close by day because it will never be night there. [26] They will bring the glory and honor of the nations into it. [27] Nothing unclean will ever enter it, nor anyone who does what is detestable or false, but only those written in the Lamb's book of life.

11.30.2020

WRITE A PRAYER BEGINNING WITH:

JESUS, YOU BRING LIGHT TO OUR WORLD.

The darkness cannot overcome the light that you bring. You illuminate the dark places of my heart and make me a vessel for your light. Please shine your light in my life and reveal any dark places and hidden character defects that still need addressed. Make my world bright and full of life!

Read Ephesians 5:8–14 again. What does it look like to reflect the light of Christ in your life and community?

I will full of righteousness, goodness, and truth towards other people. I will refrain from being involved in fruitless & ungodly works & wake up to the truth that God is my light & He will guide me in the darkness.

THE LORD WILL BE YOUR EVERLASTING LIGHT.
ISAIAH 60:19

DAY
03

TO DO WHAT
ADAM COULD NOT

GENESIS 3:1-10

THE TEMPTATION AND THE FALL

¹ Now the serpent was the most cunning of all the wild animals that the LORD God had made. He said to the woman, "Did God really say, 'You can't eat from any tree in the garden'?"

² The woman said to the serpent, "We may eat the fruit from the trees in the garden. ³ But about the fruit of the tree in the middle of the garden, God said, 'You must not eat it or touch it, or you will die.'"

⁴ "No! You will certainly not die," the serpent said to the woman. ⁵ "In fact, God knows that when you eat it your eyes will be opened and you will be like God, knowing good and evil." ⁶ The woman saw that the tree was good for food and delightful to look at, and that it was desirable for obtaining wisdom. So she took some of its fruit and ate it; she also gave some to her husband, who was with her, and he ate it. ⁷ Then the eyes of both of them were opened, and they knew they were naked; so they sewed fig leaves together and made coverings for themselves.

SIN'S CONSEQUENCES

⁸ Then the man and his wife heard the sound of the LORD God walking in the garden at the time of the evening breeze, and they hid from the LORD God among the trees of the garden. ⁹ So the LORD God called out to the man and said to him, "Where are you?"

¹⁰ And he said, "I heard you in the garden, and I was afraid because I was naked, so I hid."

MATTHEW 4:1-11

THE TEMPTATION OF JESUS

¹ Then Jesus was led up by the Spirit into the wilderness to be tempted by the devil. ² After he had fasted forty days and forty nights, he was hungry. ³ Then the tempter approached him and said, "If you are the Son of God, tell these stones to become bread."

⁴ He answered, "It is written: Man must not live on bread alone but on every word that comes from the mouth of God."

I'm always struck by the fact that God called out to Adam and Adam had to respond. Adam had responsibility to come to God, but God invited him.

5 Then the devil took him to the holy city, had him stand on the pinnacle of the temple, 6 and said to him, "If you are the Son of God, throw yourself down. For it is written:

> He will give his angels orders
>   concerning you,
> and they will support you with their hands
> so that you will not strike
> your foot against a stone."

7 Jesus told him, "It is also written: Do not test the Lord your God."

8 Again, the devil took him to a very high mountain and showed him all the kingdoms of the world and their splendor. 9 And he said to him, "I will give you all these things if you will fall down and worship me."

10 Then Jesus told him, "Go away, Satan! For it is written: Worship the Lord your God, and serve only him."

11 Then the devil left him, and angels came and began to serve him.

ROMANS 5:12-21

DEATH THROUGH ADAM AND LIFE THROUGH CHRIST

12 Therefore, just as sin entered the world through one man, and death through sin, in this way death spread to all people, because all sinned. 13 In fact, sin was in the world before the law, but sin is not charged to a person's account when there is no law. 14 Nevertheless, death reigned from Adam to Moses, even over those who did not sin in the likeness of Adam's transgression. He is a type of the Coming One.

15 But the gift is not like the trespass. For if by the one man's trespass the many died, how much more have the grace of God and the gift which comes through the grace of the one man Jesus Christ overflowed to the many. 16 And the gift is not like the one man's sin, because from one sin came the judgment, resulting in condemnation, but from many trespasses came the gift, resulting in justification. 17 If by the one man's trespass, death reigned through that one man, how much more will those who receive the overflow of grace and the gift of righteousness reign in life through the one man, Jesus Christ.

18 So then, as through one trespass there is condemnation for everyone, so also through one righteous act there is justification leading to life for everyone. 19 For just as through one man's disobedience the many were made sinners, so also through the one man's obedience the many will be made righteous. 20 The law came along to multiply the trespass. But where sin multiplied, grace multiplied even more 21 so that, just as sin reigned in death, so also grace will reign through righteousness, resulting in eternal life through Jesus Christ our Lord.

1 CORINTHIANS 15:45-49

45 So it is written, The first man Adam became a living being; the last Adam became a life-giving spirit. 46 However, the spiritual is not first, but the natural, then the spiritual.

47 The first man was from the earth, a man of dust; the second man is from heaven. 48 Like the man of dust, so are those who are of the dust; like the man of heaven, so are those who are of heaven. 49 And just as we have borne the image of the man of dust, we will also bear the image of the man of heaven.

12.01.2020

WRITE A PRAYER BEGINNING WITH:

JESUS, YOU DID WHAT ADAM COULD NOT.

You took all the sin of the world on you because you were the perfect sacrifice. Please keep me focused on you and remind me of my need for you by showing me the daily sacrifices I need to make for you. I am like Adam - weak and ashamed. Please make me more like Jesus - strong and bold. Amen.

How does Christ's perfect obedience free you to live in obedience to Him this Advent season?

It frees me by showing me the way to true joy and peace - through obedience to His teachings and by following His example. I want to be obedient to Him this Advent season so that I can be a better husband for Leslie & father for the kids.

THROUGH THE ONE MAN'S OBEDIENCE THE MANY WILL BE MADE RIGHTEOUS.
ROMANS 5:19

TO BLESS THE NATIONS

GENESIS 12:1-3

THE CALL OF ABRAM

¹ The LORD said to Abram:

> Go from your land,
> your relatives,
> and your father's house
> to the land that I will show you.
> ² I will make you into a great nation,
> I will bless you,
> I will make your name great,
> and you will be a blessing.
> ³ I will bless those who bless you,
> I will curse anyone who treats you with contempt,
> and all the peoples on earth
> will be blessed through you.

ACTS 3:17-25

¹⁷ And now, brothers and sisters, I know that you acted in ignorance, just as your leaders also did. ¹⁸ In this way God fulfilled what he had predicted through all the prophets—that his Messiah would suffer. ¹⁹ Therefore repent and turn back, so that your sins may be wiped out, ²⁰ that seasons of refreshing may come from the presence of the Lord, and that he may send Jesus, who has been appointed for you as the Messiah. ²¹ Heaven must receive him until the time of the restoration of all things, which God spoke about through his holy prophets from the beginning. ²² Moses said: The Lord your God will raise up for you a prophet like me from among your brothers. You must listen to everything he tells you. ²³ And everyone who does not listen to that prophet will be completely cut off from the people.

²⁴ In addition, all the prophets who have spoken, from Samuel and those after him, have also foretold these days. ²⁵ You are the sons of the prophets and of the covenant that God made with your ancestors, saying to Abraham, And all the families of the earth will be blessed through your offspring.

GALATIANS 3:7-29 NIV

⁷ Understand, then, that those who have faith are children of Abraham. ⁸ Scripture foresaw that God would justify the Gentiles by faith, and announced the gospel in advance to Abraham: "All nations will be blessed through you." ⁹ So those who rely on faith are blessed along with Abraham, the man of faith.

¹⁰ For all who rely on the works of the law are under a curse, as it is written: "Cursed is everyone who does not continue to do everything written in the Book of the Law." ¹¹ Clearly no one who relies on the law is justified before God, because "the righteous will live by faith." ¹² The law is not based on faith; on the contrary, it says, "The person who does these things will live by them." ¹³ Christ redeemed us from the curse of the law by becoming a curse for us, for it is written: "Cursed is everyone who is hung on a pole." ¹⁴ He redeemed us in order that the blessing given to Abraham might come to the Gentiles through Christ Jesus, so that by faith we might receive the promise of the Spirit.

THE LAW AND THE PROMISE

¹⁵ Brothers and sisters, let me take an example from everyday life. Just as no one can set aside or add to a human covenant that has been duly established, so it is in this case. ¹⁶ The promises were spoken to Abraham and to his seed. Scripture does not say "and to seeds," meaning many people, but "and to your seed," meaning one person, who is Christ. ¹⁷ What I mean is this: The law, introduced 430 years later, does not set aside the covenant previously established by God and thus do away with the promise. ¹⁸ For if the inheritance depends on the law, then it no longer depends on the promise; but God in his grace gave it to Abraham through a promise.

¹⁹ Why, then, was the law given at all? It was added because of transgressions until the Seed to whom the promise referred had come. The law was given through angels and entrusted to a mediator. ²⁰ A mediator, however, implies more than one party; but God is one.

²¹ Is the law, therefore, opposed to the promises of God? Absolutely not! For if a law had been given that could impart life, then righteousness would certainly have come by the law. ²² But Scripture has locked up everything under the control of sin, so that what was promised, being given through faith in Jesus Christ, might be given to those who believe.

CHILDREN OF GOD

²³ Before the coming of this faith, we were held in custody under the law, locked up until the faith that was to come would be revealed. ²⁴ So the law was our guardian until Christ came that we might be justified by faith. ²⁵ Now that this faith has come, we are no longer under a guardian.

²⁶ So in Christ Jesus you are all children of God through faith, ²⁷ for all of you who were baptized into Christ have clothed yourselves with Christ. ²⁸ There is neither Jew nor Gentile, neither slave nor free, nor is there male and female, for you are all one in Christ Jesus. ²⁹ If you belong to Christ, then you are Abraham's seed, and heirs according to the promise.

12.02.2020

WRITE A PRAYER BEGINNING WITH:

JESUS, YOU CAME TO BLESS THE NATIONS.

Where do you see God at work in your local community and among the nations? How are you participating in this work?

You knew that we could not redeem ourselves, so you sent your Son to save the lost. Thank you for blessing everyone with your love and for teaching us how to live through your example. Help me to pass your blessing on to others every day.

SO IN CHRIST JESUS YOU ARE ALL CHILDREN OF GOD THROUGH FAITH.
GALATIANS 3:26 NIV

GO, TELL IT ON THE MOUNTAIN

TEXT

UNKNOWN

TUNE

TRADITIONAL AFRICAN-
AMERICAN SPIRITUAL

John Wesley Work, Jr. is recognized as the
first to publish the hymn "Go, Tell It on the
Mountain," which appeared in Work's wide
collection of African-American spirituals.
Putting the tune and lyrics down on paper,
John gave voice to the unknown slave
who—despite his earthly enslavement—had
composed this song of victorious hope so
many years before. We chose to title this
Legacy Book *Jesus Christ Is Born* after a lyric
from this hymn because it celebrates the
good news of the God who makes Himself
known to His people, right where they are.

DAY
05

TO
FULFILL
THE
LAW

THE TEN COMMANDMENTS

¹ Then God spoke all these words:

² I am the Lᴏʀᴅ your God, who brought you out of the land of Egypt, out of the place of slavery.

³ Do not have other gods besides me.

⁴ Do not make an idol for yourself, whether in the shape of anything in the heavens above or on the earth below or in the waters under the earth. ⁵ Do not bow in worship to them, and do not serve them; for I, the Lᴏʀᴅ your God, am a jealous God, bringing the consequences of the fathers' iniquity on the children to the third and fourth generations of those who hate me, ⁶ but showing faithful love to a thousand generations of those who love me and keep my commands.

⁷ Do not misuse the name of the Lᴏʀᴅ your God, because the Lᴏʀᴅ will not leave anyone unpunished who misuses his name.

⁸ Remember the Sabbath day, to keep it holy: ⁹ You are to labor six days and do all your work, ¹⁰ but the seventh day is a Sabbath to the Lᴏʀᴅ your God. You must not do any work—you, your son or daughter, your male or female servant, your livestock, or the resident alien who is within your city gates. ¹¹ For the Lᴏʀᴅ made the heavens and the earth, the sea, and everything in them in six days; then he rested on the seventh day. Therefore the Lᴏʀᴅ blessed the Sabbath day and declared it holy.

¹² Honor your father and your mother so that you may have a long life in the land that the Lᴏʀᴅ your God is giving you.

¹³ Do not murder.

¹⁴ Do not commit adultery.

¹⁵ Do not steal.

¹⁶ Do not give false testimony against your neighbor.

¹⁷ Do not covet your neighbor's house. Do not covet your neighbor's wife, his male or female servant, his ox or donkey, or anything that belongs to your neighbor.

MATTHEW 5:17–48

CHRIST FULFILLS THE LAW

¹⁷ **"Don't think that I came to abolish the Law or the Prophets. I did not come to abolish but to fulfill.**

¹⁸ For truly I tell you, until heaven and earth pass away, not the smallest letter or one stroke of a letter will pass away from the law until all things are accomplished. ¹⁹ Therefore, whoever breaks one of the least of these commands and teaches others to do the same will be called least in the kingdom of heaven. But whoever does and teaches these commands will be called great in the kingdom of heaven. ²⁰ For I tell you, unless your righteousness surpasses that of the scribes and Pharisees, you will never get into the kingdom of heaven.

MURDER BEGINS IN THE HEART

²¹ "You have heard that it was said to our ancestors, Do not murder, and whoever murders will be subject to judgment. ²² But I tell you, everyone who is angry with his brother or sister will be subject to judgment. Whoever insults his brother or sister, will be subject to the court. Whoever says, 'You fool!' will be subject to hellfire. ²³ So if you are offering your gift on the altar, and there you remember that your brother or sister has something against you, ²⁴ leave your gift there in front of the altar. First go and be reconciled with your brother or sister, and then come and offer your gift. ²⁵ Reach a settlement quickly with your adversary while you're on the way with him to the court, or your adversary will hand you over to the judge, and the judge to the officer, and you will be thrown into prison. ²⁶ Truly I tell you, you will never get out of there until you have paid the last penny.

ADULTERY BEGINS IN THE HEART

²⁷ "You have heard that it was said, Do not commit adultery. ²⁸ But I tell you, everyone who looks at a woman lustfully has already committed adultery with her in his heart. ²⁹ If your right eye causes you to sin, gouge it out and throw it away. For it is better that you lose one of the parts

of your body than for your whole body to be thrown into hell. [30] And if your right hand causes you to sin, cut it off and throw it away. For it is better that you lose one of the parts of your body than for your whole body to go into hell.

DIVORCE PRACTICES CENSURED

[31] "It was also said, Whoever divorces his wife must give her a written notice of divorce. [32] But I tell you, everyone who divorces his wife, except in a case of sexual immorality, causes her to commit adultery. And whoever marries a divorced woman commits adultery.

TELL THE TRUTH

[33] "Again, you have heard that it was said to our ancestors, You must not break your oath, but you must keep your oaths to the Lord [34] But I tell you, don't take an oath at all: either by heaven, because it is God's throne; [35] or by the earth, because it is his footstool; or by Jerusalem, because it is the city of the great King. [36] Do not swear by your head, because you cannot make a single hair white or black. [37] But let your 'yes' mean 'yes,' and your 'no' mean 'no.' Anything more than this is from the evil one.

GO THE SECOND MILE

[38] "You have heard that it was said, An eye for an eye and a tooth for a tooth. [39] But I tell you, don't resist an evildoer. On the contrary, if anyone slaps you on your right cheek, turn the other to him also. [40] As for the one who wants to sue you and take away your shirt, let him have your coat as well. [41] And if anyone forces you to go one mile, go with him two. [42] Give to the one who asks you, and don't turn away from the one who wants to borrow from you.

LOVE YOUR ENEMIES

[43] "You have heard that it was said, Love your neighbor and hate your enemy. [44] But I tell you, love your enemies and pray for those who persecute you, [45] so that you may be children of your Father in heaven. For he causes his sun to rise on the evil and the good, and sends rain on the righteous and the unrighteous. [46] For if you love those who love you, what reward will you have? Don't even the tax collectors do the same? [47] And if you greet only your brothers and sisters, what are you doing out of the ordinary? Don't even the Gentiles do the same?

⁴⁸ Be perfect, therefore, as your heavenly Father is perfect."

ROMANS 8:1-4

THE LIFE-GIVING SPIRIT

¹ Therefore, there is now no condemnation for those in Christ Jesus, ² because the law of the Spirit of life in Christ Jesus has set you free from the law of sin and death. ³ For what the law could not do since it was weakened by the flesh, God did. He condemned sin in the flesh by sending his own Son in the likeness of sinful flesh as a sin offering, ⁴ in order that the law's requirement would be fulfilled in us who do not walk according to the flesh but according to the Spirit.

12.03.2020

WRITE A PRAYER BEGINNING WITH:

JESUS, YOU FULFILLED THE LAW.

You did what we could not do - live a perfect life and be the sacrifice for our sins. The law shows us what is wrong and what we shall not do, but does not give us the power to do what is right. You have fulfilled the law and given us the power to do what is pure, and holy, and right. Thank you, Jesus.

What does Jesus's interpretation of the Law in Matthew 5 teach you about the heart of God? How does it comfort you?

God is not only interested in our actions, but instead He is interested in our hearts. He understands that we cannot keep the commands of the law on our own, so He came to ~~abolish~~ fulfill it & replace it w/ a new law. The law of grace and mercy is now mine w/ the help of the Holy Spirit.

"DON'T THINK THAT I CAME TO ABOLISH THE LAW OR THE PROPHETS. I DID NOT COME TO ABOLISH BUT TO FULFILL."
MATTHEW 5:17

DAY
06

TO BE OUR
HIGH PRIEST

THE PRIESTLY MINISTRY INAUGURATED

¹ On the eighth day Moses summoned Aaron, his sons, and the elders of Israel. ² He said to Aaron, "Take a young bull for a sin offering and a ram for a burnt offering, both without blemish, and present them before the LORD. ³ And tell the Israelites: Take a male goat for a sin offering; a calf and a lamb, male yearlings without blemish, for a burnt offering; ⁴ an ox and a ram for a fellowship offering to sacrifice before the LORD; and a grain offering mixed with oil. For today the LORD is going to appear to you."

⁵ They brought what Moses had commanded to the front of the tent of meeting, and the whole community came forward and stood before the LORD. ⁶ Moses said, "This is what the LORD commanded you to do, that the glory of the LORD may appear to you." ⁷ Then Moses said to Aaron, "Approach the altar and sacrifice your sin offering and your burnt offering; make atonement for yourself and the people. Sacrifice the people's offering and make atonement for them, as the LORD commanded."

LEVITICUS 16:29–34

²⁹ "This is to be a permanent statute for you: In the seventh month, on the tenth day of the month you are to practice self-denial and do no work, both the native and the alien who resides among you. ³⁰ Atonement will be made for you on this day to cleanse you, and you will be clean from all your sins before the LORD. ³¹ It is a Sabbath of complete rest for you, and you must practice self-denial; it is a permanent statute. ³² The priest who is anointed and ordained to serve as high priest in place of his father will make atonement. He will put on the linen garments, the holy garments, ³³ and make atonement for the most holy place. He will make atonement for the tent of meeting and the altar and will make atonement for the priests and all the people of the assembly. ³⁴ This is to be a permanent statute for you, to make atonement for the Israelites once a year because of all their sins." And all this was done as the LORD commanded Moses.

HEBREWS 4:14–16

OUR GREAT HIGH PRIEST

¹⁴ Therefore, since we have a great high priest who has passed through the heavens—Jesus the Son of God—let us hold fast to our confession. ¹⁵ For

we do not have a high priest who is unable to sympathize with our weaknesses, but one who has been tempted in every way as we are, yet without sin. ¹⁶ Therefore, let us approach the throne of grace with boldness, so that we may receive mercy and find grace to help us in time of need.

HEBREWS 5:1-10

CHRIST, A HIGH PRIEST

¹ For every high priest taken from among men is appointed in matters pertaining to God for the people, to offer both gifts and sacrifices for sins. ² He is able to deal gently with those who are ignorant and are going astray, since he is also clothed with weakness. ³ Because of this, he must make an offering for his own sins as well as for the people. ⁴ No one takes this honor on himself; instead, a person is called by God, just as Aaron was. ⁵ In the same way, Christ did not exalt himself to become a high priest, but God who said to him,

You are my Son;
today I have become your Father,

⁶ also says in another place,

You are a priest forever
according to the order of Melchizedek.

⁷ During his earthly life, he offered prayers and appeals with loud cries and tears to the one who was able to save him from death, and he was heard because of his reverence. ⁸ Although he was the Son, he learned obedience from what he suffered. ⁹ After he was perfected, he became

the source of eternal salvation for all who obey him, ¹⁰ and he was declared by God a high priest according to the order of Melchizedek.

HEBREWS 10:10-14

¹⁰ By this will, we have been sanctified through the offering of the body of Jesus Christ once for all time.

¹¹ Every priest stands day after day ministering and offering the same sacrifices time after time, which can never take away sins. ¹² But this man, after offering one sacrifice for sins forever, sat down at the right hand of God. ¹³ He is now waiting until his enemies are made his footstool. ¹⁴ For by one offering he has perfected forever those who are sanctified.

12.04.2020

WRITE A PRAYER BEGINNING WITH:

JESUS,
YOU ARE OUR
HIGH PRIEST.

How does the truth
that Christ sympathizes
with your weaknesses and
made a once-and-for-all
offering for your sins bring
you comfort?

Because of this, you
are our mediator.
You can make intercession
to God for me. Please
do this for me, Jesus.
Please ask God to
send His Holy Spirit
to empower me to
live a better life - a
life free from deceit
and lies and depravity.
I want to experience
the freedom that comes
from fully trusting You
and being fully honest.

I have so many
weaknesses and
failures in my life.
If Jesus can really
sympathize with me
then He won't judge
me but will instead
lift me up and pray
for me and cause good
to come from my
shattered life. I am
a sinner & can't do
anything good by my
own power. I need Jesus
to be my strength and
to take my sin and
shame from me.

HE WAS DECLARED BY GOD A HIGH PRIEST.
HEBREWS 5:10

ADVENT
GAR
LANDS

Simple, classic pieces of decor like these homemade garlands go a long way in bringing a fresh and festive holiday feel to your home.

DIFFICULTY LEVEL

MATERIALS

FRESH PINES
ZIP TIES OR FLORAL WIRE
ORANGES
POPCORN
CINNAMON STICKS
EMBROIDERY NEEDLE
WAXED THREAD

PINE GARLAND

DIRECTIONS

For a pine garland, purchase or cut fresh pine branches. Use zip ties to connect each piece to the next, and drape the finished garland on your banister or mantle, or over a doorframe or windowsill.

DRIED ORANGE GARLAND

DIRECTIONS

Heat oven to 200°F.

Cut oranges into ⅛-inch slices. Arrange on baking sheet and bake 3 to 4 hours.

Thread a needle and triple knot the thread to make sure it's stable. Once the orange slices are dry, string them along the thread until your garland is your desired length. Tie off the thread with a triple knot to complete. Be sure to add a loop on each end for hanging!

POPCORN GARLAND

DIRECTIONS

Thread a needle and triple knot the end for stability. Gently thread popped popcorn onto the needle. If you puncture a spot that is too thin, the popcorn will break, so aim for the center of the popcorn.

PINE, ORANGE, AND CINNAMON GARLAND

DIRECTIONS

Follow the directions for preparing a pine garland and drying oranges above. Alternate threading dried oranges and cinnamon sticks along the waxed thread.

Use floral wire to attach the two garlands together, creating a layered look.

DAY
07

GRACE DAY

**ADVENT IS A SEASON
OF ANTICIPATION AND
CELEBRATION. WE LONG
FOR THE PROMISED
SAVIOR'S RETURN, EVEN AS
WE REJOICE THAT HE HAS
ALREADY COME TO US.**

Use this day to catch up on your reading,
pray, and reflect on the wondrous light and
hope of Christ.

FOR GOD WHO SAID, "LET LIGHT SHINE OUT OF DARKNESS," HAS SHONE IN OUR HEARTS TO GIVE THE LIGHT OF THE KNOWLEDGE OF GOD'S GLORY IN THE FACE OF JESUS CHRIST.

2 CORINTHIANS 4:6

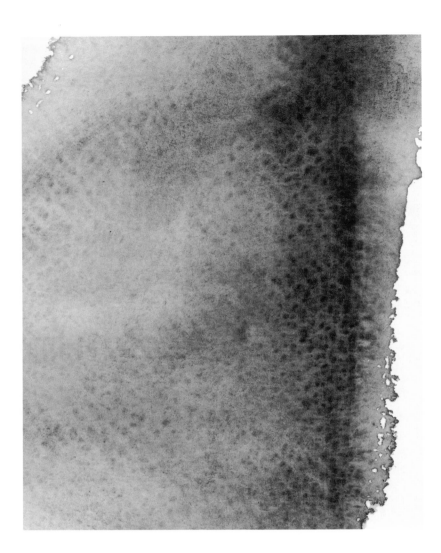

PEACE

THE SECOND SUNDAY OF ADVENT

On this second Sunday of Advent, we celebrate the peace promised to us in Christ. Spend this week memorizing or meditating on Isaiah 9:6 as you thank God for the peace found in His presence.

FOR A CHILD WILL
BE BORN FOR US,
A SON WILL BE
GIVEN TO US,
AND THE GOVERNMENT
WILL BE ON HIS
SHOULDERS.
HE WILL BE NAMED
WONDERFUL
COUNSELOR,
MIGHTY GOD,
ETERNAL FATHER,
PRINCE OF PEACE.

ISAIAH 9:6

TO TEACH US HOW TO WALK IN GOD'S WAYS

MATTHEW 5:1-12, 43-48

THE SERMON ON THE MOUNT

[1] When he saw the crowds, he went up on the mountain, and after he sat down, his disciples came to him. [2] Then he began to teach them, saying:

THE BEATITUDES

[3] "Blessed are the poor in spirit,
for the kingdom of heaven is theirs.
[4] Blessed are those who mourn,
for they will be comforted.
[5] Blessed are the humble,
for they will inherit the earth.
[6] Blessed are those who hunger and thirst
   for righteousness,
for they will be filled.
[7] Blessed are the merciful,
for they will be shown mercy.
[8] Blessed are the pure in heart,
for they will see God.
[9] Blessed are the peacemakers,
for they will be called sons of God.
[10] Blessed are those who are persecuted because
   of righteousness,
for the kingdom of heaven is theirs.

[11] "You are blessed when they insult you and persecute you and falsely say every kind of evil against you because of me. [12] Be glad and rejoice, because your reward is great in heaven. For that is how they persecuted the prophets who were before you."

…

[43] "You have heard that it was said, Love your neighbor and hate your enemy. [44] But I tell you, love your enemies and pray for those who persecute you, [45] so that you may be children of

your Father in heaven. For he causes his sun to rise on the evil and the good, and sends rain on the righteous and the unrighteous. ⁴⁶ For if you love those who love you, what reward will you have? Don't even the tax collectors do the same? ⁴⁷ And if you greet only your brothers and sisters, what are you doing out of the ordinary? Don't even the Gentiles do the same? ⁴⁸ Be perfect, therefore, as your heavenly Father is perfect."

JOHN 13:1-17

JESUS WASHES HIS DISCIPLES' FEET

¹ Before the Passover Festival, Jesus knew that his hour had come to depart from this world to the Father. Having loved his own who were in the world, he loved them to the end.

² Now when it was time for supper, the devil had already put it into the heart of Judas, Simon Iscariot's son, to betray him. ³ Jesus knew that the Father had given everything into his hands, that he had come from God, and that he was going back to God. ⁴ So he got up from supper, laid aside his outer clothing, took a towel, and tied it around himself. ⁵ Next, he poured water into a basin and began to wash his disciples' feet and to dry them with the towel tied around him.

⁶ He came to Simon Peter, who asked him, "Lord, are you going to wash my feet?"

⁷ Jesus answered him, "What I'm doing you don't realize now, but afterward you will understand."

⁸ "You will never wash my feet," Peter said.

Jesus replied, "If I don't wash you, you have no part with me."

⁹ Simon Peter said to him, "Lord, not only my feet, but also my hands and my head."

¹⁰ "One who has bathed," Jesus told him, "doesn't need to wash anything except his feet, but he is completely clean. You are clean, but not all of you." ¹¹ For he knew who would betray him. This is why he said, "Not all of you are clean."

THE MEANING OF FOOT WASHING

¹² When Jesus had washed their feet and put on his outer clothing, he reclined again and said to them, "Do you know what I have done for you? ¹³ You call me Teacher and Lord—and you are speaking rightly, since that is what I am. ¹⁴ So if I, your Lord and Teacher, have washed your feet, you also ought to wash one another's feet. ¹⁵ For I have given you an example, that you also should do just as I have done for you.

¹⁶ "Truly I tell you, a servant is not greater than his master, and a messenger is not greater than the one who sent him. ¹⁷ If you know these things, you are blessed if you do them."

1 PETER 2:21-25

²¹ For you were called to this, because Christ also suffered for you, leaving you an example, that you should follow in his steps. ²² He did not commit sin, and no deceit was found in his mouth; ²³ when he was insulted, he did not insult in return; when he suffered, he did not threaten but entrusted himself to the one who judges justly. ²⁴ He himself bore our sins in his body on the tree; so that, having died to sins, we might live for righteousness. By his wounds you have been healed. ²⁵ For you were like sheep going astray, but you have now returned to the Shepherd and Overseer of your souls.

12.07.2020

WRITE A PRAYER BEGINNING WITH:

JESUS, YOU TEACH US HOW TO WALK IN GOD'S WAYS.

Thinking both broadly and more specifically, what does it look like to model your life after Jesus's example?

You teach us what is right and pure and good. Please teach me these things and show me how to live a humble, pure life free from pride and deception. God, I am a sinner; I need your forgiveness and your help. Please help me to feel your heart and teach me to love Leslie the way you love her & the way you love all of your childeren.

Jesus was connected to the Father everyday, so I need to commit to prayer & Bible study everyday. Jesus was unselfish and always put others above himself. I need to do the same, especially for Leslie and the kids. Jesus was honest in all His dealings. Jesus was empathetic and showed emotion when others were hurting.

"FOR I HAVE GIVEN YOU AN EXAMPLE, THAT YOU ALSO SHOULD DO JUST AS I HAVE DONE FOR YOU."

JOHN 13:15

DAY
10

TO
SEEK
AND
SAVE
THE
LOST

8 This is what the LORD says:

> I will answer you in a time of favor,
> and I will help you in the day of salvation.
> I will keep you, and I will appoint you
> to be a covenant for the people,
> to restore the land,
> to make them possess the desolate inheritances,
> 9 saying to the prisoners, "Come out,"
> and to those who are in darkness, "Show yourselves."
> They will feed along the pathways,
> and their pastures will be on all the barren heights.
> 10 They will not hunger or thirst,
> the scorching heat or sun will not strike them;
> for their compassionate one will guide them,
> and lead them to springs.
> 11 I will make all my mountains into a road,
> and my highways will be raised up.
> 12 See, these will come from far away,
> from the north and from the west,
> and from the land of Sinim.
>
> 13 Shout for joy, you heavens!
> Earth, rejoice!
> Mountains break into joyful shouts!
> For the LORD has comforted his people,
> and will have compassion on his afflicted ones.

MATTHEW 9:9-13

9 As Jesus went on from there, he saw a man named Matthew sitting at the tax office, and he said to him, "Follow me," and he got up and followed him.

10 While he was reclining at the table in the house, many tax collectors and sinners came to eat with Jesus and his disciples. 11 When the Pharisees saw this, they asked his disciples, "Why does your teacher eat with tax collectors and sinners?"

12 Now when he heard this, he said, "It is not those who are well who need a doctor, but those who are sick. 13 Go and learn what this means: I desire mercy and not sacrifice. For I didn't come to call the righteous, but sinners."

REJECTION AT NAZARETH

16 He came to Nazareth, where he had been brought up. As usual, he entered the synagogue on the Sabbath day and stood up to read. 17 The scroll of the prophet Isaiah was given to him, and unrolling the scroll, he found the place where it was written:

18 The Spirit of the Lord is on me,
because he has anointed me
to preach good news to the poor.
He has sent me
to proclaim release to the captives
and recovery of sight to the blind,
to set free the oppressed,
19 to proclaim the year of the Lord's favor.

20 He then rolled up the scroll, gave it back to the attendant, and sat down. And the eyes of everyone in the synagogue were fixed on him. 21 He began by saying to them, "Today as you listen, this Scripture has been fulfilled."

22 They were all speaking well of him and were amazed by the gracious words that came from his mouth; yet they said, "Isn't this Joseph's son?"

23 Then he said to them, "No doubt you will quote this proverb to me: 'Doctor, heal yourself. What we've heard that took place in Capernaum, do here in your hometown also.'"

24 He also said, "Truly I tell you, no prophet is accepted in his hometown. 25 But I say to you, there were certainly many widows in Israel in Elijah's days, when the sky was shut up for three years and six months while a great famine came over all the land. 26 Yet Elijah was not sent to any of them except a widow at Zarephath in Sidon. 27 And in the prophet Elisha's time, there were many in Israel who had leprosy, and yet not one of them was cleansed except Naaman the Syrian."

28 When they heard this, everyone in the synagogue was enraged. 29 They got up, drove him out of town, and brought him to the edge of the hill that their town was built on, intending to hurl him over the cliff. 30 But he passed right through the crowd and went on his way.

JESUS VISITS ZACCHAEUS

1 He entered Jericho and was passing through. 2 There was a man named Zacchaeus who was a chief tax collector, and he was rich. 3 He was trying to see who Jesus was, but he was not able because of the crowd, since he was a short man. 4 So running ahead, he climbed up a sycamore tree to see Jesus, since he was about to pass that way. 5 When Jesus came to the place, he looked up and said to him, "Zacchaeus, hurry and come down because today it is necessary for me to stay at your house."

6 So he quickly came down and welcomed him joyfully. 7 All who saw it began to complain, "He's gone to stay with a sinful man."

8 But Zacchaeus stood there and said to the Lord, "Look, I'll give half of my possessions to the poor, Lord. And if I have extorted anything from anyone, I'll pay back four times as much."

9 "Today salvation has come to this house," Jesus told him, "because he too is a son of Abraham. 10 For the Son of Man has come to seek and to save the lost."

12.08.2020

WRITE A PRAYER BEGINNING WITH:

JESUS, YOU CAME TO SEEK AND SAVE THE LOST.

Jesus regularly sought out those society rejected. How has Jesus sought you? How can you demonstrate the radical love of Jesus to people in your life?

You truly found me when I was lost. I knew I was lost and couldn't find my way out. You came to me and have been leading me out of my desperate situation. You have sought me, and now I am asking that you would continue saving me. Please make me more like you!
Amen.

In my depraved state, there was no way I could have found Jesus. He found me and freed me from the chains of my addiction and is slowly, painfully making me more like Him. I can share His work in my life now with others so they can journey w/ me and help me.

"FOR THE SON OF MAN HAS COME TO SEEK AND TO SAVE THE LOST."
LUKE 19:10

COME, THOU LONG-EXPECTED JESUS

TEXT

CHARLES WESLEY

MUSIC

ROWLAND H. PRICHARD

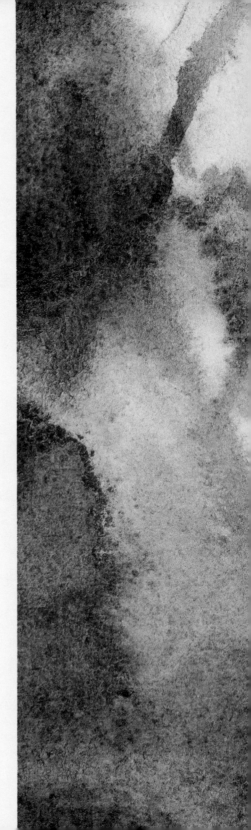

1. Come, Thou long - ex - pect - ed Je - sus, Born to set Thy
2. Born Thy peo - ple to de - liv - er, Born a child, and

peo - ple free; From our fears and sins re - lease us;
yet a King, Born to reign in us for - ev - er,

Let us find our rest in Thee. Is - rael's strength and con - so -
Now Thy gra - cious king - dom bring. By Thine own e - ter - nal

la - tion, Hope of all the earth Thou art; Dear de - sire of
Spir - it rule in all our hearts a - lone; By Thine all - suf -

ev - 'ry na - tion, Joy of ev - 'ry long - ing heart.
fi - cient mer - it, Raise us to Thy glo - rious throne.

DAY
11

TO REIGN **AS** KING FOREVER

[8] "So now this is what you are to say to my servant David: 'This is what the LORD of Armies says: I took you from the pasture, from tending the flock, to be ruler over my people Israel. [9] I have been with you wherever you have gone, and I have destroyed all your enemies before you. I will make a great name for you like that of the greatest on the earth. [10] I will designate a place for my people Israel and plant them, so that they may live there and not be disturbed again. Evildoers will not continue to oppress them as they have done [11] ever since the day I ordered judges to be over my people Israel. I will give you rest from all your enemies.

"'The LORD declares to you: The LORD himself will make a house for you. [12] When your time comes and you rest with your ancestors, I will raise up after you your descendant, who will come from your body, and I will establish his kingdom. [13] He is the one who will build a house for my name, and I will establish the throne of his kingdom forever. [14] I will be his father, and he will be my son. When he does wrong, I will discipline him with a rod of men and blows from mortals. [15] But my faithful love will never leave him as it did when I removed it from Saul, whom I removed from before you. [16] Your house and kingdom will endure before me forever, and your throne will be established forever.'"

ISAIAH 11:1-6

REIGN OF THE DAVIDIC KING

[1] Then a shoot will grow from the stump of Jesse,
and a branch from his roots will bear fruit.
[2] The Spirit of the LORD will rest on him—
a Spirit of wisdom and understanding,
a Spirit of counsel and strength,
a Spirit of knowledge and of the fear of the LORD.
[3] His delight will be in the fear of the LORD.
He will not judge
by what he sees with his eyes,
he will not execute justice
by what he hears with his ears,
[4] but he will judge the poor righteously
and execute justice for the oppressed of the land.
He will strike the land
with a scepter from his mouth,

and he will kill the wicked
with a command from his lips.
⁵ Righteousness will be a belt around his hips;
faithfulness will be a belt around his waist.

⁶ The wolf will dwell with the lamb,
and the leopard will lie down with the goat.
The calf, the young lion, and the fattened calf
   will be together,
and a child will lead them.

MATTHEW 12:22-23

A HOUSE DIVIDED

²² Then a demon-possessed man who was blind and unable to speak was brought to him. He healed him, so that the man could both speak and see. ²³ All the crowds were astounded and said, "Could this be the Son of David?"

MATTHEW 22:41-46

THE QUESTION ABOUT THE MESSIAH

⁴¹ While the Pharisees were together, Jesus questioned them, ⁴² "What do you think about the Messiah? Whose son is he?"

They replied, "David's."

⁴³ He asked them, "How is it then that David, inspired by the Spirit, calls him 'Lord':

   ⁴⁴ The Lord declared to my Lord,
   'Sit at my right hand
   until I put your enemies under your feet'?

⁴⁵ "If David calls him 'Lord,' how, then, can he be his son?" ⁴⁶ No one was able to answer him at all, and from that day no one dared to question him anymore.

ACTS 2:29-36

²⁹ Brothers and sisters, I can confidently speak to you about the patriarch David: He is both dead and buried, and his tomb is with us to this day. ³⁰ Since he was a prophet, he knew that God had sworn an oath to him to seat one of his descendants on his throne. ³¹ Seeing what was to come, he spoke concerning the resurrection of the Messiah: He was not abandoned in Hades, and his flesh did not experience decay.

³² God has raised this Jesus; we are all witnesses of this. ³³ Therefore, since he has been exalted to the right hand of God and has received from the Father the promised Holy Spirit, he has poured out what you both see and hear. ³⁴ For it was not David who ascended into the heavens, but he himself says:

   The Lord declared to my Lord,
   "Sit at my right hand
   ³⁵ until I make your enemies your footstool."

³⁶ Therefore let all the house of Israel know with certainty that God has made this Jesus, whom you crucified, both Lord and Messiah.

HEBREWS 1:3-4

³ The Son is the radiance of God's glory and the exact expression of his nature, sustaining all things by his powerful word. After making purification for sins, he sat down at the right hand of the Majesty on high. ⁴ So he became superior to the angels, just as the name he inherited is more excellent than theirs.

12.09.2020

WRITE A PRAYER BEGINNING WITH:

JESUS, YOU
REIGN AS KING.

You deserve our adoration and praise. You deserve our reverance and obedience. LORD, please cut down anything in my life that is not pleasing to you, my King. Jesus, rule over my life, rule over every moment, rule over my relationships. Jesus, you command my love and obedience forever.

How does remembering that Christ reigns as King affect the way you live?

It should make me desire to please Him in everything I do. The King has the ability to give good gifts as well as take things away. I want to be worthy of the good gifts He gives me.

"I WILL ESTABLISH THE THRONE OF HIS KINGDOM FOREVER."
2 SAMUEL 7:13

TO BRING GOD'S KINGDOM TO EARTH

DANIEL 2:27–45

[27] Daniel answered the king, "No wise man, medium, magician, or diviner is able to make known to the king the mystery he asked about. [28] But there is a God in heaven who reveals mysteries, and he has let King Nebuchadnezzar know what will happen in the last days. Your dream and the visions that came into your mind as you lay in bed were these: [29] Your Majesty, while you were in your bed, thoughts came to your mind about what will happen in the future. The revealer of mysteries has let you know what will happen. [30] As for me, this mystery has been revealed to me, not because I have more wisdom than anyone living, but in order that the interpretation might be made known to the king, and that you may understand the thoughts of your mind.

THE DREAM'S INTERPRETATION

[31] "Your Majesty, as you were watching, suddenly a colossal statue appeared. That statue, tall and dazzling, was standing in front of you, and its appearance was terrifying. [32] The head of the statue was pure gold, its chest and arms were silver, its stomach and thighs were bronze, [33] its legs were iron, and its feet were partly iron and partly fired clay. [34] As you were watching, a stone broke off without a hand touching it, struck the statue on its feet of iron and fired clay, and crushed them. [35] Then the iron, the fired clay, the bronze, the silver, and the gold were shattered and became like chaff from the summer threshing floors. The wind carried them away, and not a trace of them could be found. But the stone that struck the statue became a great mountain and filled the whole earth.

[36] "This was the dream; now we will tell the king its interpretation. [37] Your Majesty, you are king of kings. The God of the heavens has given you sovereignty, power, strength, and glory. [38] Wherever people live—or wild animals, or birds of the sky—he has handed them over to you and made you ruler over them all. You are the head of gold.

[39] "After you, there will arise another kingdom, inferior to yours, and then another, a third kingdom, of bronze, which will rule the whole earth. [40] A fourth kingdom will be as strong as iron; for iron crushes and shatters everything, and like iron that smashes, it will crush and smash all the others. [41] You saw the feet and toes, partly of a potter's fired clay and partly of iron—it will be a divided kingdom, though some of the strength of iron will be in it. You saw the iron mixed with clay, [42] and that the toes of the feet were partly iron and partly fired clay—part of the kingdom will be strong, and part will be brittle. [43] You saw the iron mixed with clay—the peoples will mix with one another but will not hold together, just as iron does not mix with fired clay.

[44] "In the days of those kings, the God of the heavens will set up a kingdom that will never be destroyed, and this kingdom will not be left to another people. It will crush all these kingdoms and bring them to an end, but will itself endure forever. [45] You saw a stone break off from the mountain without a hand touching it, and it crushed the iron, bronze, fired clay, silver, and gold. The great God has told the king what will happen in the future. The dream is certain, and its interpretation reliable."

DANIEL 7:13-14

[13] I continued watching in the night visions,

and suddenly one like a son of man
was coming with the clouds of heaven.
He approached the Ancient of Days
and was escorted before him.

**[14] He was given dominion
and glory and a kingdom,
so that those of every people,
nation, and language
should serve him.**

His dominion is an everlasting dominion
that will not pass away,
and his kingdom is one
that will not be destroyed.

MATTHEW 6:7–13

⁷ When you pray, don't babble like the Gentiles, since they imagine they'll be heard for their many words. ⁸ Don't be like them, because your Father knows the things you need before you ask him.

THE LORD'S PRAYER

⁹ "Therefore, you should pray like this:

Our Father in heaven,
your name be honored as holy.
¹⁰ Your kingdom come.
Your will be done
on earth as it is in heaven.
¹¹ Give us today our daily bread.
¹² And forgive us our debts,
as we also have forgiven our debtors.
¹³ And do not bring us into temptation,
but deliver us from the evil one.

MARK 1:14–15

¹⁴ After John was arrested, Jesus went to Galilee, proclaiming the good news of God: ¹⁵ "The time is fulfilled, and the kingdom of God has come near. Repent and believe the good news!"

JOHN 18:36

"My kingdom is not of this world," said Jesus. "If my kingdom were of this world, my servants would fight, so that I wouldn't be handed over to the Jews. But as it is, my kingdom is not from here."

REVELATION 11:15

The seventh angel blew his trumpet, and there were loud voices in heaven saying,

The kingdom of the world has become the kingdom of our Lord and of his Christ,

and he will reign forever and ever.

12.10.2020

WRITE A PRAYER BEGINNING WITH:

JESUS, YOU CAME TO BRING GOD'S KINGDOM TO EARTH.

God's kingdom on earth is what we should long for. Jesus, please show me the way to having that longing for your kingdom when you will rule as a just leader who knows & sees all. Right now I am too scared of that to long for it, but I want You to help me change that.

Name an area of your life where you can pursue God's kingdom values. How does knowing that Jesus came to bring God's kingdom to earth change the way you celebrate the Advent season?

I want to learn to be totally truthful and recognize when I am not. Knowing that Jesus came to bring God's kingdom should give me an earnesty to make changes.

"YOUR KINGDOM COME. YOUR WILL BE DONE ON EARTH AS IT IS IN HEAVEN."
MATTHEW 6:10

THE SEASONS
OF THE CHURCH

The Advent season is one part of the larger Church calendar, a centuries-old way many Christian denominations order the year. Structured around the moving date of Easter Sunday and the fixed date of Christmas, the liturgical Church year consists of six seasons as well as ordinary time.

EPIPHANY

WHAT IS IT?
Epiphany comes from a Greek word that means "to manifest" or "to show." It is also known as the Feast of the Three Kings, Three Kings' Day, and Twelfth Night. Epiphany commemorates the arrival of the magi in Bethlehem and is a reminder that Christ's birth is good news for all.

WHEN IS IT?
January 6, twelve days after Christmas. Some traditions celebrate this season through the Sunday before Ash Wednesday.

KEY SCRIPTURE
Mt 2:1–11

CHRISTMASTIDE

WHAT IS IT?
A season celebrating the birth of Jesus.

WHEN IS IT?
December 25 through January 5, also known as the Twelve Days of Christmas or Yuletide.

KEY SCRIPTURES
Is 9:2–7; Mt 1:18–24;
Lk 1:26–38; 2:1–20

ADVENT

WHAT IS IT?
A season of anticipating the celebration of Jesus's birth. The term *advent* comes from a Latin word meaning "coming" or "arrival."

WHEN IS IT?
Four Sundays before Christmas Day through December 24.

LENT

WHAT IS IT?
A solemn season of self-reflection, repentance, and Scripture meditation as a means of preparing hearts and minds to celebrate Easter. Many traditions observe Lent by fasting—traditionally by abstaining from eating meat, fish, eggs, and fat, though many contemporary Christians will instead give up one "luxury" item during Lent.

WHEN IS IT?
Ash Wednesday through Holy Saturday, forty fasting days and six feasting Sundays.

KEY SCRIPTURE
Lk 4:1-13

EASTERTIDE

WHAT IS IT?
A celebration of Jesus Christ's resurrection from the dead, the central belief of the Christian faith. Eastertide is the culmination of both Lent and the week leading up to Easter, which is referred to as Holy Week.

WHEN IS IT?
Easter Sunday through the day before Pentecost. At seven weeks, it is the longest formal season of the Church year.

KEY SCRIPTURES
Lk 24:1-12, 36-53; Jn 11:25-26

PENTECOST

WHAT IS IT?
A celebration of when the Holy Spirit descended on believers from all over the world who were gathered in Jerusalem. It marks the birthday of the Christian Church.

WHEN IS IT?
The seventh Sunday after Easter.

KEY SCRIPTURE
Ac 2:1-41

ORDINARY TIME

Most of the Church year consists of ordinary time, the period between Pentecost and Advent, and Epiphany and Lent. Though the colors used to mark the liturgical year differ from denomination to denomination, ordinary time is always green.

DAY
13

TO DEFEAT THE ENEMY

I will put hostility between you and the woman,
and between your offspring and her offspring.
He will strike your head,
and you will strike his heel.

MARK 3:22-27

²² The scribes who had come down from Jerusalem said, "He is possessed by Beelzebul," and, "He drives out demons by the ruler of the demons."

²³ So he summoned them and spoke to them in parables: "How can Satan drive out Satan? ²⁴ If a kingdom is divided against itself, that kingdom cannot stand. ²⁵ If a house is divided against itself, that house cannot stand. ²⁶ And if Satan opposes himself and is divided, he cannot stand but is finished. ²⁷ But no one can enter a strong man's house and plunder his possessions unless he first ties up the strong man. Then he can plunder his house."

1 CORINTHIANS 15:24-26

²⁴ Then comes the end, when he hands over the kingdom to God the Father, when he abolishes all rule and all authority and power. ²⁵ For he must reign until he puts all his enemies under his feet. ²⁶ The last enemy to be abolished is death.

HEBREWS 2:5-18

JESUS AND HUMANITY

⁵ For he has not subjected to angels the world to come that we are talking about. ⁶ But someone somewhere has testified:

What is man that you remember him,
or the son of man that you care for him?
⁷ You made him lower than the angels
for a short time;
you crowned him with glory and honor
⁸ and subjected everything under his feet.

For in subjecting everything to him, he left nothing that is not subject to him. As it is, we do not yet see everything subjected to him. ⁹ But we do see Jesus—made lower than the angels for a short time so that by God's grace he might taste death for everyone—crowned with glory and honor because he suffered death.

¹⁰ For in bringing many sons and daughters to glory, it was entirely appropriate that God—for whom and through whom all things exist—should make the pioneer of their salvation perfect through sufferings. ¹¹ For the one who sanctifies and those who are sanctified all have one Father. That is why Jesus is not ashamed to call them brothers and sisters, ¹² saying:

> I will proclaim your name to my brothers and sisters;
> I will sing hymns to you in the congregation.

¹³ Again, I will trust in him. And again, Here I am with the children God gave me.

¹⁴ Now since the children have flesh and blood in common, Jesus also shared in these, so that through his death he might destroy the one holding the power of death—that is, the devil— ¹⁵ and free those who were held in slavery all their lives by the fear of death. ¹⁶ For it is clear that he does not reach out to help angels, but to help Abraham's offspring. ¹⁷ Therefore, he had to be like his brothers and sisters in every way, so that he could become a merciful and faithful high priest in matters pertaining to God, to make atonement for the sins of the people. ¹⁸ For since he himself has suffered when he was tempted, he is able to help those who are tempted.

1 JOHN 3:7–10

⁷ Little children, let no one deceive you. The one who does what is right is righteous, just as he is righteous. ⁸ The one who commits sin is of the devil, for the devil has sinned from the beginning. The Son of God was revealed for this purpose: to destroy the devil's works. ⁹ Everyone who has been born of God does not sin, because his seed remains in him; he is not able to sin, because he has been born of God. ¹⁰ This is how God's children and the devil's children become obvious. Whoever does not do what is right is not of God, especially the one who does not love his brother or sister.

REVELATION 12:10–12

¹⁰ Then I heard a loud voice in heaven say,

> The salvation and the power
> and the kingdom of our God
> and the authority of his Christ
> have now come,
> because the accuser of our brothers
>   and sisters,
> who accuses them
> before our God day and night,
> has been thrown down.
> ¹¹ They conquered him
> by the blood of the Lamb
> and by the word of their testimony;
> for they did not love their lives
> to the point of death.
> ¹² Therefore rejoice, you heavens,
> and you who dwell in them!
> Woe to the earth and the sea,
> because the devil has come down to you
> with great fury,
> because he knows his time is short.

12.11.2020

WRITE A PRAYER BEGINNING WITH:

JESUS, YOU'VE DEFEATED THE ENEMY.

Now I ask you to defeat the enemy in me. Jesus, the enemy is strong and my depravity is deep. I am recognizing that I don't even know the full extent of deceit and manipulation I am capable of. I ask you to please come close to me and search me and reveal the deep defects that are still in me so that, by your power, they may be defeated.

How does Jesus's victory over the devil empower you to resist temptation?

It gives me confidence that I can overcome, with this help, any temptation or difficult circumstance the devil throws my way. Victory over my deceitful and manipulative ways is possible!

THE SON OF GOD WAS REVEALED FOR THIS PURPOSE:
TO DESTROY THE DEVIL'S WORKS.
1 JOHN 3:8

WINTER STROOPWAFELS

DIFFICULTY LEVEL

PREP TIME	WAFELS	CARAMEL FILLING
15 MIN	1 ¼ cups all-purpose flour	1 cup sugar
	1 teaspoon baking powder	1 tablespoon light corn syrup
COOK TIME	¼ teaspoon kosher salt	¼ cup water
15 MIN	2 large eggs	⅓ cup heavy cream
	¾ cup white sugar	1 teaspoon vanilla extract
YIELD	2 teaspoons vanilla extract	1 tablespoon unsalted butter
12 WAFELS	½ teaspoon lemon extract	½ teaspoon salt
	⅓ cup unsalted butter, melted and cooled	

DIRECTIONS

Preheat a nonstick, electric waffle-cone iron.

In a medium bowl, whisk together flour, baking powder, and salt. Set aside.

In the bowl of an electric mixer fitted with the whisk attachment, beat eggs. Whisk in sugar until well combined, then add extracts. Slowly whisk in cooled butter in a steady stream until the batter is smooth.

Gradually add the flour mixture and whisk until thoroughly combined.

Spoon batter into 2-inch circles onto the center of the heated waffle-cone iron. Close the lid and cook for 90 seconds.*

Carefully remove the cooked wafel from the iron and transfer to a cutting board. Use a round cookie cutter to cut off the edges for a perfectly circular wafel. Working quickly while the wafel is still hot, gently slice it horizontally using a sharp knife.

Place on a wire rack to cool. Repeat until all of the batter is cooked.

For the caramel filling, combine sugar, corn syrup, and water in a medium saucepan. Cook over medium heat until sugar dissolves and liquid becomes a dark amber color, about 10 minutes.

Reduce heat to low and slowly add cream, stirring until combined. Add vanilla, butter, and salt. Stir until smooth.

Place a generous tablespoon of caramel on the bottom wafel half. Top with the other wafel half and gently push down until the caramel spreads to the edges. Repeat until all wafels are filled.

Stroopwafels are traditionally placed on top of a hot drink, allowing the steam from the drink to warm the caramel inside.

Time will vary based on the temperature of your waffle-cone iron.

DAY
14

GRACE
DAY

ADVENT IS A SEASON
OF ANTICIPATION AND
CELEBRATION. WE LONG FOR
THE PROMISED SAVIOR'S
RETURN, EVEN AS WE REJOICE
THAT HE HAS ALREADY COME
TO US.

Use this day to catch up on your reading, pray,
and reflect on the wondrous light and peace
of Christ.

"TODAY SALVATION HAS COME TO THIS HOUSE," JESUS TOLD HIM, "BECAUSE HE TOO IS A SON OF ABRAHAM. FOR THE SON OF MAN HAS COME TO SEEK AND TO SAVE THE LOST."

LUKE 19:9–10

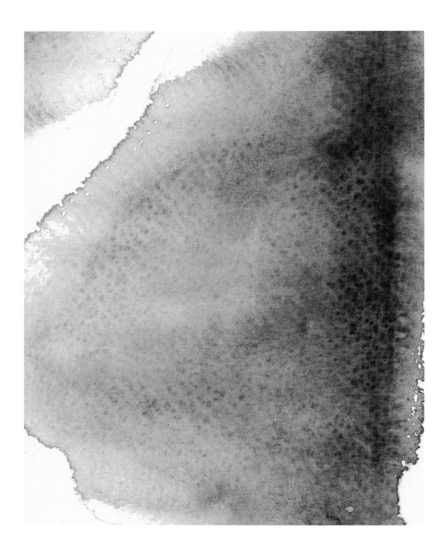

THE THIRD SUNDAY OF ADVENT

On this third Sunday of Advent, we rejoice in the coming of Christ our King. Spend this week memorizing or meditating on Luke 2:10-11 as you thank God for the joy He gives us and the joy yet to come.

BUT THE ANGEL SAID
TO THEM, "DON'T BE
AFRAID, FOR LOOK, I
PROCLAIM TO YOU
GOOD NEWS OF GREAT
JOY THAT WILL BE FOR
ALL THE PEOPLE: TODAY
IN THE CITY OF DAVID
A SAVIOR WAS BORN
FOR YOU, WHO IS THE
MESSIAH, THE LORD."

LUKE 2:10–11

DAY 16

TO SHOW US
PERFECT LOVE

For God loved the world in this way: He gave his one and only Son, so that everyone who believes in him will not perish but have eternal life.

JOHN 15:9–17

CHRISTLIKE LOVE

⁹ "As the Father has loved me, I have also loved you. Remain in my love.

¹⁰ If you keep my commands you will remain in my love, just as I have kept my Father's commands and remain in his love.

¹¹ "I have told you these things so that my joy may be in you and your joy may be complete.

¹² "This is my command: Love one another as I have loved you.

¹³ No one has greater love than this: to lay down his life for his friends. ¹⁴ You are my friends if you do what I command you.

¹⁵ I do not call you servants anymore, because a servant doesn't know what his master is doing. I have called you friends, because I have made known to you everything I have heard from my Father. ¹⁶ You did not choose me, but I chose you. I appointed you to go and produce fruit and that your fruit should remain, so that whatever you ask the Father in my name, he will give you.

¹⁷ "This is what I command you: Love one another."

ROMANS 5:6–11

THE JUSTIFIED ARE RECONCILED

⁶ For while we were still helpless, at the right time, Christ died for the ungodly. ⁷ For rarely will someone die for a just person—though for a good person perhaps someone might even dare to die. ⁸ But God proves his own love for us in that while we were still sinners, Christ died for us. ⁹ How much more then, since we have now been justified by his blood,

will we be saved through him from wrath. [10] For if, while we were enemies, we were reconciled to God through the death of his Son, then how much more, having been reconciled, will we be saved by his life. [11] And not only that, but we also boast in God through our Lord Jesus Christ, through whom we have now received this reconciliation.

1 JOHN 4:7–21

KNOWING GOD THROUGH LOVE

[7] Dear friends, let us love one another, because love is from God, and everyone who loves has been born of God and knows God. [8] The one who does not love does not know God, because God is love. [9] God's love was revealed among us in this way: God sent his one and only Son into the world so that we might live through him. [10] Love consists in this: not that we loved God, but that he loved us and sent his Son to be the atoning sacrifice for our sins. [11] Dear friends, if God loved us in this way, we also must love one another. [12] No one has ever seen God. If we love one another, God remains in us and his love is made complete in us. [13] This is how we know that we remain in him and he in us: He has given us of his Spirit. [14] And we have seen and we testify that the Father has sent his Son as the world's Savior. [15] Whoever confesses that Jesus is the Son of God—God remains in him and he in God. [16] And we have come to know and to believe the love that God has for us.

God is love, and the one who remains in love remains in God, and God remains in him. [17] In this, love is made complete with us so that we may have confidence in the day of judgment, because as he is, so also are we in this world. [18] There is no fear in love; instead, perfect love drives out fear, because fear involves punishment. So the one who fears is not complete in love.

[19] **We love because he first loved us.**

[20] If anyone says, "I love God," and yet hates his brother or sister, he is a liar. For the person who does not love his brother or sister whom he has seen cannot love God whom he has not seen. [21] And we have this command from him: The one who loves God must also love his brother and sister.

12.14.2020

WRITE A PRAYER BEGINNING WITH:

JESUS, YOU CAME TO SHOW US PERFECT LOVE.

How does Jesus continue to show you perfect love as you walk in relationship with Him? What are ways you can love your brothers and sisters in Christ during this Advent season?

Before you came, the world did not know what perfect love was. Now that you have shown me, please help me to love others, starting with my wife. Jesus, my humble prayer is that you would help me to see Leslie as you see her all the time. Please help me love her w/ all that is in me, the way you love the church.

Jesus does not turn me away even in my sin and depravity. His love does not depend on me doing anything for Him. I would like to love Leslie by giving her the time, space, and understanding she needs during this difficult period of her life.

WE LOVE BECAUSE HE FIRST LOVED US.
1 JOHN 4:19

TO HEAL OUR WOUNDS

ISAIAH 52:13–15

THE SERVANT'S SUFFERING AND EXALTATION

¹³ See, my servant will be successful;
he will be raised and lifted up and greatly exalted.
¹⁴ Just as many were appalled at you—
his appearance was so disfigured
that he did not look like a man,
and his form did not resemble a human being—
¹⁵ so he will sprinkle many nations.
Kings will shut their mouths because of him,
for they will see what had not been told them,
and they will understand what they had not heard.

ISAIAH 53:1–12

¹ Who has believed what we have heard?
And to whom has the arm of the LORD
    been revealed?
² He grew up before him like a young plant
and like a root out of dry ground.
He didn't have an impressive form
or majesty that we should look at him,
no appearance that we should desire him.
³ He was despised and rejected by men,
a man of suffering who knew what sickness was.
He was like someone people turned away from;
he was despised, and we didn't value him.

⁴ Yet he himself bore our sicknesses,
and he carried our pains;
but we in turn regarded him stricken,

struck down by God, and afflicted.

[5] But he was pierced because of our rebellion,

crushed because of our iniquities;

punishment for our peace was on him,

and we are healed by his wounds.

[6] We all went astray like sheep;

we all have turned to our own way;

and the LORD has punished him

for the iniquity of us all.

[7] He was oppressed and afflicted,

yet he did not open his mouth.

Like a lamb led to the slaughter

and like a sheep silent before her shearers,

he did not open his mouth.

[8] He was taken away because of oppression and judgment,

and who considered his fate?

For he was cut off from the land of the living;

he was struck because of my people's rebellion.

[9] He was assigned a grave with the wicked,

but he was with a rich man at his death,

because he had done no violence

and had not spoken deceitfully.

[10] Yet the LORD was pleased to crush him severely.

When you make him a guilt offering,

he will see his seed, he will prolong his days,

and by his hand, the LORD's pleasure will be accomplished.

[11] After his anguish,

he will see light and be satisfied.

By his knowledge,

my righteous servant will justify many,

and he will carry their iniquities.

[12] Therefore I will give him the many as a portion,

and he will receive the mighty as spoil,

because he willingly submitted to death,

and was counted among the rebels;

yet he bore the sin of many

and interceded for the rebels.

²⁹ Moving on from there, Jesus passed along the Sea of Galilee. He went up on a mountain and sat there, ³⁰ and large crowds came to him, including the lame, the blind, the crippled, those unable to speak, and many others.

They put them at his feet, and he healed them.

LUKE 5:17-25

THE SON OF MAN FORGIVES AND HEALS

¹⁷ On one of those days while he was teaching, Pharisees and teachers of the law were sitting there who had come from every village of Galilee and Judea, and also from Jerusalem. And the Lord's power to heal was in him. ¹⁸ Just then some men came, carrying on a stretcher a man who was paralyzed. They tried to bring him in and set him down before him. ¹⁹ Since they could not find a way to bring him in because of the crowd, they went up on the roof and lowered him on the stretcher through the roof tiles into the middle of the crowd before Jesus.

²⁰ Seeing their faith he said, "Friend, your sins are forgiven."

²¹ Then the scribes and the Pharisees began to think to themselves, "Who is this man who speaks blasphemies? Who can forgive sins but God alone?"

²² But perceiving their thoughts, Jesus replied to them, "Why are you thinking this in your hearts? ²³ Which is easier: to say, 'Your sins are forgiven,' or to say, 'Get up and walk'? ²⁴ But so that you may know that the Son of Man has authority on earth to forgive sins"—he told the paralyzed man, "I tell you: Get up, take your stretcher, and go home."

²⁵ Immediately he got up before them, picked up what he had been lying on, and went home glorifying God.

THE SOURCE OF LIFE

¹ Then he showed me the river of the water of life, clear as crystal, flowing from the throne of God and of the Lamb ² down the middle of the city's main street. The tree of life was on each side of the river, bearing twelve kinds of fruit, producing its fruit every month.

The leaves of the tree are for healing the nations, ³ and there will no longer be any curse.

The throne of God and of the Lamb will be in the city, and his servants will worship him. ⁴ They will see his face, and his name will be on their foreheads. ⁵ Night will be no more; people will not need the light of a lamp or the light of the sun, because the Lord God will give them light, and they will reign forever and ever.

12.15.2020

WRITE A PRAYER BEGINNING WITH:

JESUS,
YOU HEAL
OUR WOUNDS.

What physical or emotional wound can you bring before Jesus today? How do these passages bring you comfort?

You were wounded so that we could be healed. You offer your healing to us, all we need to do is take it. Please take my life and my ~~scars~~ wounds and heal them. Please leave the scars so that I may never forget your healing power.

I want to suffer for righteousness' sake, not for being disobedient and sinful. I am an unclean sinner, and I want Jesus to heal me from the wounds of my past behaviors and I also want Him to heal those I love. Healing takes time and effort, and I am ready to do what the Great Healer prescribes in order to get better.

WE ARE HEALED BY HIS WOUNDS.
ISAIAH 53:5

TO BE THE LAMB OF GOD

INSTRUCTIONS FOR THE PASSOVER

¹ The LORD said to Moses and Aaron in the land of Egypt, ² "This month is to be the beginning of months for you; it is the first month of your year. ³ Tell the whole community of Israel that on the tenth day of this month they must each select an animal of the flock according to their fathers' families, one animal per family. ⁴ If the household is too small for a whole animal, that person and the neighbor nearest his house are to select one based on the combined number of people; you should apportion the animal according to what each will eat. ⁵ You must have an unblemished animal, a year-old male; you may take it from either the sheep or the goats. ⁶ You are to keep it until the fourteenth day of this month; then the whole assembly of the community of Israel will slaughter the animals at twilight. ⁷ They must take some of the blood and put it on the two doorposts and the lintel of the houses where they eat them. ⁸ They are to eat the meat that night; they should eat it, roasted over the fire along with unleavened bread and bitter herbs. ⁹ Do not eat any of it raw or cooked in boiling water, but only roasted over fire—its head as well as its legs and inner organs. ¹⁰ You must not leave any of it until morning; any part of it left until morning you must burn. ¹¹ Here is how you must eat it: You must be dressed for travel, your sandals on your feet, and your staff in your hand. You are to eat it in a hurry; it is the LORD's Passover.

¹² "I will pass through the land of Egypt on that night and strike every firstborn male in the land of Egypt, both people and animals. I am the LORD; I will execute judgments against all the gods of Egypt. ¹³ The blood on the houses where you are staying will be a distinguishing mark for you; when I see the blood, I will pass over you. No plague will be among you to destroy you when I strike the land of Egypt.

¹⁴ "This day is to be a memorial for you, and you must celebrate it as a festival to the LORD. You are to celebrate it throughout your generations as a permanent statute."

...

²¹ Then Moses summoned all the elders of Israel and said to them, "Go, select an animal from the flock according to your families, and slaughter the Passover animal. ²² Take a cluster of hyssop, dip it in the blood that is in the basin, and brush the lintel and the two doorposts with some of the blood in the basin. None of you may go out the door of his house until

morning. [23] When the Lord passes through to strike Egypt and sees the blood on the lintel and the two doorposts, he will pass over the door and not let the destroyer enter your houses to strike you.

[24] "Keep this command permanently as a statute for you and your descendants. [25] When you enter the land that the Lord will give you as he promised, you are to observe this ceremony. [26] When your children ask you, 'What does this ceremony mean to you?' [27] you are to reply, 'It is the Passover sacrifice to the Lord, for he passed over the houses of the Israelites in Egypt when he struck the Egyptians, and he spared our homes.'" So the people knelt low and worshiped. [28] Then the Israelites went and did this; they did just as the Lord had commanded Moses and Aaron.

JOHN 1:29

The next day John saw Jesus coming toward him and said, "Look, the Lamb of God, who takes away the sin of the world!"

1 CORINTHIANS 5:6-8

[6] Your boasting is not good. Don't you know that a little leaven leavens the whole batch of dough? [7] Clean out the old leaven so that you may be a new unleavened batch, as indeed you are. For Christ our Passover lamb has been sacrificed. [8] Therefore, let us observe the feast, not with old leaven or with the leaven of malice and evil, but with the unleavened bread of sincerity and truth.

1 PETER 1:17-21

[17] If you appeal to the Father who judges impartially according to each one's work, you are to conduct yourselves in reverence during your time living as strangers. [18] For you know that you were redeemed from your empty way of life inherited from your ancestors, not with perishable things like silver or gold, [19] but with the precious blood of Christ, like that of an unblemished and spotless lamb. [20] He was foreknown before the foundation of the world but was revealed in these last times for you. [21] Through him you believe in God, who raised him from the dead and gave him glory, so that your faith and hope are in God.

12.16.2020

WRITE A PRAYER BEGINNING WITH:

JESUS, YOU ARE THE LAMB OF GOD.

You were unblemished and innocent, yet you were sacrificed for me in order to take my sins away from me and set me free from my evil desires and wicked ways. Please help me to build routines and sacred practices into my life, like the Passover, that remind me daily of the sacrifice that was made for me even while I was empty & a sinner.

In light of Exodus 12, why is it significant that Jesus is called the Lamb of God?

Because it reflects the way that a lamb was used to nourish the Israelites and to save the Israelites from death. In the same way, Jesus' sacrifice takes the penalty of death from me and gives me life-sustaining nourishment.

LOOK, THE LAMB OF GOD, WHO TAKES AWAY THE SIN OF THE WORLD!
JOHN 1:29

CHRIST AS PROPHET, PRIEST, AND KING

The Old Testament records the narratives of many prophets, priests, and kings of old whose lives pointed God's people to the coming Messiah. During the season of Advent, we turn to Scripture to remember and rejoice that Jesus Christ took on each of these unique roles of authority and fulfilled them perfectly as no one else could. Even today, Immanuel, "God is with us," still serves with perfect love and justice as our perfect Prophet, Priest, and King.

PROPHET

LONG AGO GOD SPOKE TO OUR ANCESTORS BY THE PROPHETS AT DIFFERENT TIMES AND IN DIFFERENT WAYS. IN THESE LAST DAYS, HE HAS SPOKEN TO US BY HIS SON.

HEBREWS 1:1–2

A PROPHET...

- Speaks on behalf of God to His people.
- Declares the truth of God's living Word.
- Proclaims God's coming judgment on His people, calling them to repent and turn away from sin.
- Inspires vision and hope for lasting restoration.

In the Old Testament, prophets were set apart to deliver God's Word. One of their main roles was to proclaim God's coming judgment, highlighting both the discipline and healing that would come to God's people in need of salvation. Because Jesus Christ was both a messenger of redemption and the means through which it was accomplished, He is above all other prophets.

TODAY
Jesus is our perfect Prophet. He calls us to share in the work of proclaiming a message of salvation and mercy secured through His life, death, and resurrection.

REFERENCES:

IS 7:14; 9:6–7; JR 1:5–10; MT 5:17; 16:15

PRIEST

A PRIEST...

- Represents God before His people and His people before their God.

- Cares for the sacred space where God's presence dwells.

- Calls for people to worship God and models this practice.

- Intercedes for God's people through prayer and sacrifice.

In the Old Testament, priests tended to the tabernacle where the presence of God dwelled. They worked to anchor God's people in the practice of worship and brought imperfect sacrifices for imperfect people before a Holy God, asking Him to forgive them. There was no chair for the priests in the temple because their work was never done. But God's throne room is a more perfect tabernacle with a chair for our High Priest, Jesus.

TODAY

Christ is the perfect Priest. He brought us peace with God by offering Himself up as the perfect, substitutionary sacrifice and asks us to share in the work of interceding for others.

REFERENCES:

EX 25:8–22; NM 18:6–7; 28:11; GL 6:2; HEB 4:16

KING

AT THE NAME OF JESUS EVERY KNEE SHOULD BOW, IN HEAVEN AND ON EARTH AND UNDER THE EARTH, AND EVERY TONGUE CONFESS THAT JESUS CHRIST IS LORD, TO THE GLORY OF GOD THE FATHER.

PHILIPPIANS 2:10–11 ESV

A KING...

- Represents the people before both God and other nations.

- Defends the kingdom in battle, laying down his life in sacrificial service.

- Rules God's people with justice and righteousness.

- Observes and protects the covenant between God and His people.

In the Old Testament, kings had the choice to follow God's commands and covenants, which led to His blessing, or reject Him and suffer the consequences along with their people. Although Jesus came to earth in the humblest way imaginable, He was born King of the Jews, or more specifically, King of the people of God. All authority in heaven and on earth has been given to Him, and He conquers the enemy, protects us, and makes us into God's people.

TODAY

Christ is the perfect King. He calls us to share in His holy work of defending and serving others who bear the image of God.

REFERENCES:

MT 28:18; 2TH 3:3; HEB 6:10; RV 19:16

DAY 19

TO BE THE FIRSTFRUITS OF THE RESURRECTION

² Many who sleep in the dust
of the earth will awake,
some to eternal life,
and some to disgrace and eternal contempt.
³ Those who have insight will shine
like the bright expanse of the heavens,
and those who lead many to righteousness,
like the stars forever and ever.

JOHN 11:17-27

THE RESURRECTION AND THE LIFE

¹⁷ When Jesus arrived, he found that Lazarus had already been in the tomb four days. ¹⁸ Bethany was near Jerusalem (less than two miles away). ¹⁹ Many of the Jews had come to Martha and Mary to comfort them about their brother.

²⁰ As soon as Martha heard that Jesus was coming, she went to meet him, but Mary remained seated in the house. ²¹ Then Martha said to Jesus, "Lord, if you had been here, my brother wouldn't have died. ²² Yet even now I know that whatever you ask from God, God will give you."

²³ "Your brother will rise again," Jesus told her.

²⁴ Martha said to him, "I know that he will rise again in the resurrection at the last day."

²⁵ Jesus said to her, "I am the resurrection and the life. The one who believes in me, even if he dies, will live. ²⁶ Everyone who lives and believes in me will never die. Do you believe this?"

²⁷ "Yes, Lord," she told him, "I believe you are the Messiah, the Son of God, who comes into the world."

JOHN 20:1-18

THE EMPTY TOMB

¹ On the first day of the week Mary Magdalene came to the tomb early, while it was still dark. She saw that the stone had been removed from the

tomb. [2] So she went running to Simon Peter and to the other disciple, the one Jesus loved, and said to them, "They've taken the Lord out of the tomb, and we don't know where they've put him!"

[3] At that, Peter and the other disciple went out, heading for the tomb. [4] The two were running together, but the other disciple outran Peter and got to the tomb first. [5] Stooping down, he saw the linen cloths lying there, but he did not go in. [6] Then, following him, Simon Peter also came. He entered the tomb and saw the linen cloths lying there. [7] The wrapping that had been on his head was not lying with the linen cloths but was folded up in a separate place by itself. [8] The other disciple, who had reached the tomb first, then also went in, saw, and believed. [9] For they did not yet understand the Scripture that he must rise from the dead. [10] Then the disciples returned to the place where they were staying.

MARY MAGDALENE SEES THE RISEN LORD

[11] But Mary stood outside the tomb, crying. As she was crying, she stooped to look into the tomb. [12] She saw two angels in white sitting where Jesus's body had been lying, one at the head and the other at the feet. [13] They said to her, "Woman, why are you crying?"

"Because they've taken away my Lord," she told them, "and I don't know where they've put him."

[14] Having said this, she turned around and saw Jesus standing there, but she did not know it was Jesus. [15] "Woman," Jesus said to her, "why are you crying? Who is it that you're seeking?"

Supposing he was the gardener, she replied, "Sir, if you've carried him away, tell me where you've put him, and I will take him away."

[16] Jesus said to her, "Mary."

Turning around, she said to him in Aramaic, "*Rabboni*!"—which means "Teacher."

[17] "Don't cling to me," Jesus told her, "since I have not yet ascended to the Father. But go to my brothers and tell them that I am ascending to my Father and your Father, to my God and your God."

¹⁸ Mary Magdalene went and announced to the disciples, "I have seen the Lord!" And she told them what he had said to her.

ROMANS 8:34

Who is the one who condemns? Christ Jesus is the one who died, but even more, has been raised; he also is at the right hand of God and intercedes for us.

1 CORINTHIANS 15:12–20, 35–44, 50–57

RESURRECTION ESSENTIAL TO THE FAITH

¹² Now if Christ is proclaimed as raised from the dead, how can some of you say, "There is no resurrection of the dead"? ¹³ If there is no resurrection of the dead, then not even Christ has been raised; ¹⁴ and if Christ has not been raised, then our proclamation is in vain, and so is your faith. ¹⁵ Moreover, we are found to be false witnesses about God, because we have testified wrongly about God that he raised up Christ—whom he did not raise up, if in fact the dead are not raised. ¹⁶ For if the dead are not raised, not even Christ has been raised. ¹⁷ And if Christ has not been raised, your faith is worthless; you are still in your sins. ¹⁸ Those, then, who have fallen asleep in Christ have also perished. ¹⁹ If we have put our hope in Christ for this life only, we should be pitied more than anyone.

CHRIST'S RESURRECTION GUARANTEES OURS

²⁰ But as it is, Christ has been raised from the dead, the firstfruits of those who have fallen asleep.

…

THE NATURE OF THE RESURRECTION BODY

³⁵ But someone will ask, "How are the dead raised? What kind of body will they have when they come?" ³⁶ You fool! What you sow does not come to life unless it dies. ³⁷ And as for what you sow—you are not sowing the body that will be, but only a seed, perhaps of wheat or another grain. ³⁸ But God gives it a body as he wants, and to each of the seeds its own body. ³⁹ Not all flesh is the same flesh; there is one flesh for humans, another for animals, another for birds, and another for fish. ⁴⁰ There are heavenly bodies and earthly bodies, but the splendor of the heavenly bodies is different from that of the earthly ones. ⁴¹ There is a

splendor of the sun, another of the moon, and another of the stars; in fact, one star differs from another star in splendor. [42] So it is with the resurrection of the dead: Sown in corruption, raised in incorruption; [43] sown in dishonor, raised in glory; sown in weakness, raised in power; [44] sown a natural body, raised a spiritual body. If there is a natural body, there is also a spiritual body.

...

VICTORIOUS RESURRECTION

[50] What I am saying, brothers and sisters, is this: Flesh and blood cannot inherit the kingdom of God, nor can corruption inherit incorruption. [51] Listen, I am telling you a mystery: We will not all fall asleep, but we will all be changed, [52] in a moment, in the twinkling of an eye, at the last trumpet. For the trumpet will sound, and the dead will be raised incorruptible, and we will be changed. [53] For this corruptible body must be clothed with incorruptibility, and this mortal body must be clothed with immortality. [54] When this corruptible body is clothed with incorruptibility, and this mortal body is clothed with immortality, then the saying that is written will take place:

Death has been swallowed up in victory.
[55] Where, death, is your victory?
Where, death, is your sting?

[56] The sting of death is sin, and the power of sin is the law. [57] But thanks be to God, who gives us the victory through our Lord Jesus Christ!

COLOSSIANS 1:18

He is also the head of the body, the church;
he is the beginning,
the firstborn from the dead,
so that he might come to have
first place in everything.

12.17.2020

WRITE A PRAYER BEGINNING WITH:

JESUS, YOU CAME TO BE THE FIRSTFRUITS OF THE RESURRECTION.

You did not stay dead, but are raised from the dead. You will someday physically raise me from the dead so that I can live in your presence forever. I pray that you would raise me from my spiritual death in this life and help me to be alive and vibrant as a child of God.

> How does knowing that Jesus defeated death and sits alive at God's right hand give you hope for both life now and life after death?

Jesus is powerful and able to accomplish anything. He can change me from the evil person I am now into a new and beautiful person. I can trust that He will do it, but I also need to couple that trust with action and perseverance.

JESUS SAID TO HER, "I AM THE RESURRECTION AND THE LIFE."
JOHN 11:25

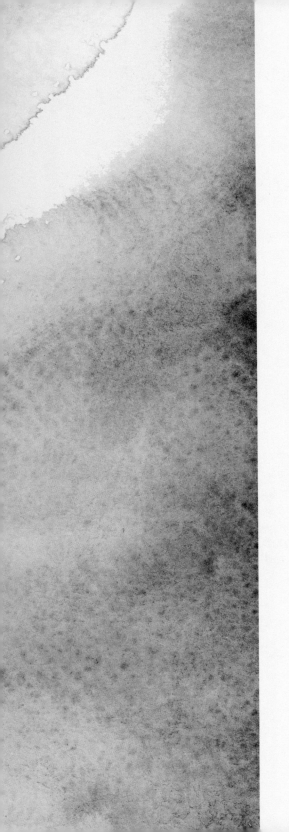

ANGELS WE HAVE HEARD ON HIGH

TEXT

TRADITIONAL FRENCH CAROL

MUSIC

TRADITIONAL FRENCH MELODY; LAST
STANZA SETTING AND CHORAL ENDING
BY DAVID HUNTSINGER

1. An - gels we have heard on high, Sweet-ly sing-ing o'er the plains;
2. Shep-herds, why this ju - bi - lee? Why your joy-ous strains pro - long?
3. Come to Beth - le - hem, and see Him whose birth the an - gels sing;
4. See with - in a man-ger laid Je - sus, Lord of heav'n and earth!

And the moun-tains in re - ply, Ech - o back their joy - ous strains.
Say what may the tid - ings be which in-spire your heav'n - ly song?
Come, a - dore on bend - ed knee Christ the Lord, the new - born King.
Ma - ry, Jo - seph, lend your aid, With us sing our Sav - ior's birth.

Chorus

Glo - ri - a in ex-cel-sis De-o!

Glo - ri - a in ex-cel-sis De - o!

Optional last stanza setting

Unison

4. See with - in a man - ger laid Je - sus, Lord of heav'n and earth!

Ma - ry, Jo - seph, lend your aid, With us sing our Sav - ior's birth.

Chorus
Sing parts

Glo - - - - ri - a

in ex-cel-sis De - o! Glo - - -

- ri - a in ex-cel-sis De - o!

Ending
molto rit.

Extended choral ending
rit.
a little slower

De - o! In ex-cel-sis

De - o! Glo-ri-a!

113

TO MAKE ALL THINGS NEW

ROMANS 8:18–30

FROM GROANS TO GLORY

[18] For I consider that the sufferings of this present time are not worth comparing with the glory that is going to be revealed to us. [19] For the creation eagerly waits with anticipation for God's sons to be revealed. [20] For the creation was subjected to futility—not willingly, but because of him who subjected it—in the hope [21] that the creation itself will also be set free from the bondage to decay into the glorious freedom of God's children. [22] For we know that the whole creation has been groaning together with labor pains until now. [23] Not only that, but we ourselves who have the Spirit as the firstfruits—we also groan within ourselves, eagerly waiting for adoption, the redemption of our bodies. [24] Now in this hope we were saved, but hope that is seen is not hope, because who hopes for what he sees? [25] Now if we hope for what we do not see, we eagerly wait for it with patience.

[26] In the same way the Spirit also helps us in our weakness, because we do not know what to pray for as we should, but the Spirit himself intercedes for us with inexpressible groanings. [27] And he who searches our hearts knows the mind of the Spirit, because he intercedes for the saints according to the will of God.

[28] We know that all things work together for the good of those who love God, who are called according to his purpose. [29] For those he foreknew he also predestined to be conformed to the image of his Son, so that he would be the firstborn among many brothers and sisters. [30] And those he predestined, he also called; and those he called, he also justified; and those he justified, he also glorified.

2 CORINTHIANS 5:11-21

[11] Therefore, since we know the fear of the Lord, we try to persuade people. What we are is plain to God, and I hope it is also plain to your consciences. [12] We are not commending ourselves to you again, but giving you an opportunity to be proud of us, so that you may have a reply for those who take pride in outward appearance rather than in the heart. [13] For if we are out of our mind, it is for God; if we are in our right mind, it is for you. [14] For the love of Christ compels us, since we have reached this conclusion, that one died for all, and therefore all died. [15] And he died for all so that those who live should no longer live for themselves, but for the one who died for them and was raised.

THE MINISTRY OF RECONCILIATION

[16] From now on, then, we do not know anyone from a worldly perspective. Even if we have known Christ from a worldly perspective, yet now we no longer know him in this way. [17] Therefore, if anyone is in Christ, he is a new creation; the old has passed away, and see, the new has come! [18] Everything is from God, who has reconciled us to himself through Christ and has given us the ministry of reconciliation. [19] That is, in Christ, God was reconciling the world to himself, not counting their trespasses against them, and he has committed the message of reconciliation to us.

[20] Therefore, we are ambassadors for Christ, since God is making his appeal through us. We plead on Christ's behalf, "Be reconciled to God." [21] He made the one who did not know sin to be sin for us, so that in him we might become the righteousness of God.

REVELATION 21:1-7

THE NEW CREATION

[1] Then I saw a new heaven and a new earth; for the first heaven and the first earth had passed away, and the sea was no more. [2] I also saw the holy city, the new Jerusalem, coming down out of heaven from God, prepared like a bride adorned for her husband.

[3] Then I heard a loud voice from the throne: Look, God's dwelling is with humanity, and he will live with them. They will be his peoples, and God himself will be with them and will be their God. [4] He will wipe away every tear from their eyes. Death will be no more; grief, crying, and pain will be no more, because the previous things have passed away.

[5] Then the one seated on the throne said, "Look, I am making everything new." He also said, "Write, because these words are faithful and true." [6] Then he said to me, "It is done! I am the Alpha and the Omega, the beginning and the end. I will freely give to the thirsty from the spring of the water of life. [7] The one who conquers will inherit these things, and I will be his God, and he will be my son."

12.18.2020

WRITE A PRAYER BEGINNING WITH:

JESUS, YOU MAKE ALL THINGS NEW.

You are making me new right now. Thank you, Jesus, for this second chance at marriage and love and acceptance and intimacy. Please help me to be grateful for it — I am grateful for it — so that I do not forget that You are the source of everything good and new.

In what areas of life do you find yourself longing for the renewal of all things? How does what you read today frame your anticipation of Christmas morning?

I pray that Christmas morning could be a rebirth for me. A rebirth from lying and deceit and disconnection into truth, humility, and intimate knowledge of Leslie.

"LOOK, I AM MAKING EVERYTHING NEW."
REVELATION 21:5

SHEPHERD'S PIE

DIFFICULTY LEVEL

 ◆ ◇ ◇

COOK TIME

30 MIN

SERVES

8–10

MEAT FILLING

2 tablespoons olive oil

1 medium yellow onion, coarsely chopped

1 pound 85/15 ground beef or ground lamb

2 teaspoons dried or fresh parsley leaves

1 teaspoon dried or fresh rosemary leaves

1 teaspoon dried or fresh thyme leaves

½ teaspoon salt

½ teaspoon ground black pepper

1 tablespoon Worcestershire sauce

2 garlic cloves, minced

2 tablespoons all-purpose flour

2 tablespoons tomato paste

1 cup beef broth

1 cup frozen mixed peas & carrots

½ cup frozen corn kernels

POTATO TOPPING

1 ½ to 2 pounds russet potatoes (about 2 large potatoes), peeled and cut into cubes

8 tablespoons unsalted butter

½ cup half & half

½ teaspoon garlic powder

¼ cup parmesan cheese

½ teaspoon salt

¼ teaspoon pepper

Flake salt and fresh thyme, for garnish

DIRECTIONS

Heat oil in a large skillet over medium-high heat. Add onions and sauté 5 minutes.

Add the ground meat to the skillet and break apart with a wooden spoon. Add the parsley, rosemary, thyme, salt, and pepper. Cook for 6 to 8 minutes, until the meat is browned, stirring occasionally.

Add Worcestershire sauce and garlic. Stir to combine. Cook for 1 minute.

Add flour and tomato paste. Stir until well incorporated.

Add broth and frozen vegetables. Bring to a boil then reduce to simmer for 5 minutes, stirring occasionally.

Set the meat mixture aside. Preheat oven to 400° F.

Place the diced potatoes in a large pot and cover with water. Bring water to a boil, then reduce to a simmer. Cook until potatoes are fork tender, 10 to 15 minutes.

Drain the potatoes in a colander, then add to the bowl of a stand mixer.

Add butter, half & half, garlic powder, parmesan, salt, and pepper. Mash the potatoes and stir until all the ingredients are well incorporated.

Layer meat mixture into the bottom of a 9x9 baking dish (or six 6-inch ramekins).

Spoon mashed potatoes on top of the meat, carefully spreading into an even covering.

If the baking dish is full, place it on a rimmed baking sheet so that the filling doesn't bubble over into your oven.

Bake uncovered for 25 to 30 minutes. Cool for 15 minutes before serving.

Garnish with flake salt and thyme.

DAY
21

GRACE
DAY

**ADVENT IS A SEASON
OF ANTICIPATION AND
CELEBRATION. WE LONG
FOR THE PROMISED
SAVIOR'S RETURN, EVEN AS
WE REJOICE THAT HE HAS
ALREADY COME TO US.**

Use this day to catch up on your reading,
pray, and reflect on the wondrous light and
joy of Christ.

YET HE HIMSELF
BORE OUR SICKNESSES,
AND HE CARRIED
OUR PAINS;
BUT WE IN TURN
REGARDED HIM
STRICKEN,
STRUCK DOWN BY GOD,
AND AFFLICTED.
BUT HE WAS PIERCED
BECAUSE OF OUR
REBELLION,
CRUSHED BECAUSE OF
OUR INIQUITIES;
PUNISHMENT FOR OUR
PEACE WAS ON HIM,
AND WE ARE HEALED BY
HIS WOUNDS.

ISAIAH 53:4–5

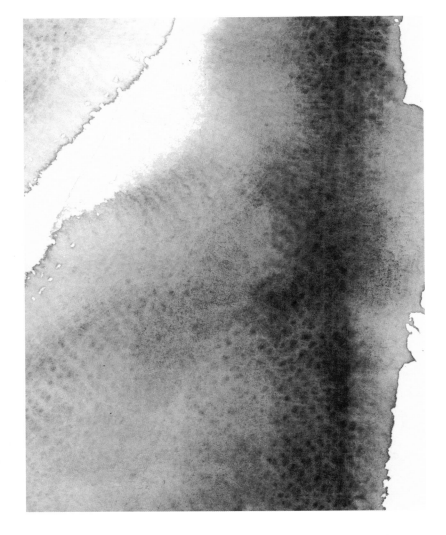

LOVE

THE FOURTH SUNDAY OF ADVENT

On this fourth Sunday of Advent, we acknowledge the sacrificial love that Christ demonstrated for us. Take this week to memorize or meditate on 1 John 4:9 as you thank God for sending His Son to rescue us from our sin and reconcile us to Himself, bringing us into right and everlasting relationship with Him.

GOD'S LOVE WAS
REVEALED AMONG US
IN THIS WAY: GOD SENT
HIS ONE AND ONLY SON
INTO THE WORLD SO
THAT WE MIGHT LIVE
THROUGH HIM.

1 JOHN 4:9

TO BE

GOD WITH US

JEREMIAH 23:5-8

THE RIGHTEOUS BRANCH OF DAVID

⁵ "Look, the days are coming"—this is the Lord's declaration—
"when I will raise up a Righteous Branch for David.
He will reign wisely as king
and administer justice and righteousness in the land.

⁶ In his days Judah will be saved,
and Israel will dwell securely.
This is the name he will be called:
The Lord Is Our Righteousness.

⁷ "Look, the days are coming"—the Lord's declaration—"when it will no longer be said, 'As the Lord lives who brought the Israelites from the land of Egypt,' ⁸ but, 'As the Lord lives, who brought and led the descendants of the house of Israel from the land of the north and from all the other countries where I had banished them.' They will dwell once more in their own land."

MATTHEW 1

THE GENEALOGY OF JESUS CHRIST

¹ An account of the genealogy of Jesus Christ, the Son of David, the Son of Abraham:

From Abraham to David
² Abraham fathered Isaac,
Isaac fathered Jacob,
Jacob fathered Judah and his brothers,
³ Judah fathered Perez and Zerah by Tamar,
Perez fathered Hezron,
Hezron fathered Aram,

⁴ Aram fathered Amminadab,

Amminadab fathered Nahshon,

Nahshon fathered Salmon,

⁵ Salmon fathered Boaz by Rahab,

Boaz fathered Obed by Ruth,

Obed fathered Jesse,

⁶ and Jesse fathered King David.

FROM DAVID TO THE BABYLONIAN EXILE

David fathered Solomon by Uriah's wife,

⁷ Solomon fathered Rehoboam,

Rehoboam fathered Abijah,

Abijah fathered Asa,

⁸ Asa fathered Jehoshaphat,

Jehoshaphat fathered Joram,

Joram fathered Uzziah,

⁹ Uzziah fathered Jotham,

Jotham fathered Ahaz,

Ahaz fathered Hezekiah,

¹⁰ Hezekiah fathered Manasseh,

Manasseh fathered Amon,

Amon fathered Josiah,

¹¹ and Josiah fathered Jeconiah and his brothers

at the time of the exile to Babylon.

FROM THE EXILE TO THE MESSIAH

¹² After the exile to Babylon

Jeconiah fathered Shealtiel,

Shealtiel fathered Zerubbabel,

¹³ Zerubbabel fathered Abiud,

Abiud fathered Eliakim,

Eliakim fathered Azor,

¹⁴ Azor fathered Zadok,

Zadok fathered Achim,

Achim fathered Eliud,

¹⁵ Eliud fathered Eleazar,

Eleazar fathered Matthan,

Matthan fathered Jacob,

¹⁶ and Jacob fathered Joseph the husband of Mary, who gave birth to Jesus who is called the Messiah.

¹⁷ So all the generations from Abraham to David were fourteen generations; and from David until the exile to Babylon, fourteen generations; and from the exile to Babylon until the Messiah, fourteen generations.

THE NATIVITY OF THE MESSIAH

¹⁸ The birth of Jesus Christ came about this way: After his mother Mary had been engaged to Joseph, it was discovered before they came together that she was pregnant from the Holy Spirit. ¹⁹ So her husband, Joseph, being a righteous man, and not wanting to disgrace her publicly, decided to divorce her secretly.

²⁰ But after he had considered these things, an angel of the Lord appeared to him in a dream, saying, "Joseph, son of David, don't be afraid to take Mary as your wife, because what has been conceived in her is from the Holy Spirit.

²¹ She will give birth to a son, and you are to name him Jesus, because he will save his people from their sins."

²² Now all this took place to fulfill what was spoken by the Lord through the prophet:

> ²³ See, the virgin will become pregnant
> and give birth to a son,
> and they will name him Immanuel,

which is translated "God is with us."

²⁴ When Joseph woke up, he did as the Lord's angel had commanded him. He married her ²⁵ but did not have sexual relations with her until she gave birth to a son. And he named him Jesus.

REVELATION 22:16

"I, Jesus, have sent my angel to attest these things to you for the churches. I am the Root and descendant of David, the bright morning star."

12.21.2020

WRITE A PRAYER BEGINNING WITH:

JESUS, YOU ARE GOD WITH US.

Before You came, God was distant and revealed Himself in a cloud, or at times in a person or angel, and in the law. You, Jesus, came to show us how to live by walking among us and by giving up yourself and your power over everything, you humbly taught us and bore our sins on yourself. Thank you, Jesus.

> Where do you sense God's presence in your life today? How are you making space to sit in His presence as Christmas Day approaches?

God's presence sort of comes and goes throughout the day. I sense it most strongly when I am reading and praying in the mornings. I would like to feel His presence all day. I am drawing near to God, and I know He promises to draw near to me. I know He is with me, and I need His help everyday.

THEY WILL NAME HIM IMMANUEL, WHICH IS TRANSLATED "GOD IS WITH US."
MATTHEW 1:23

DAY
24

TO BRING
MERCY

GABRIEL PREDICTS JOHN'S BIRTH

⁵ In the days of King Herod of Judea, there was a priest of Abijah's division named Zechariah. His wife was from the daughters of Aaron, and her name was Elizabeth. ⁶ Both were righteous in God's sight, living without blame according to all the commands and requirements of the Lord. ⁷ But they had no children because Elizabeth could not conceive, and both of them were well along in years.

⁸ When his division was on duty and he was serving as priest before God, ⁹ it happened that he was chosen by lot, according to the custom of the priesthood, to enter the sanctuary of the Lord and burn incense. ¹⁰ At the hour of incense the whole assembly of the people was praying outside. ¹¹ An angel of the Lord appeared to him, standing to the right of the altar of incense. ¹² When Zechariah saw him, he was terrified and overcome with fear. ¹³ But the angel said to him, "Do not be afraid, Zechariah, because your prayer has been heard. Your wife Elizabeth will bear you a son, and you will name him John. ¹⁴ There will be joy and delight for you, and many will rejoice at his birth. ¹⁵ For he will be great in the sight of the Lord and will never drink wine or beer. He will be filled with the Holy Spirit while still in his mother's womb. ¹⁶ He will turn many of the children of Israel to the Lord their God. ¹⁷ And he will go before him in the spirit and power of Elijah, to turn the hearts of fathers to their children, and the disobedient to the understanding of the righteous, to make ready for the Lord a prepared people."

¹⁸ "How can I know this?" Zechariah asked the angel. "For I am an old man, and my wife is well along in years."

¹⁹ The angel answered him, "I am Gabriel, who stands in the presence of God, and I was sent to speak to you and tell you this good news. ²⁰ Now listen. You will become silent and unable to speak until the day these things take place, because you did not believe my words, which will be fulfilled in their proper time."

²¹ Meanwhile, the people were waiting for Zechariah, amazed that he stayed so long in the sanctuary. ²² When he did come out, he could not speak to them. Then they realized that he had seen a vision in the sanctuary. He was making signs to them and remained speechless. ²³ When the days of his ministry were completed, he went back home.

24 After these days his wife Elizabeth conceived and kept herself in seclusion for five months. She said, 25 "The Lord has done this for me. He has looked with favor in these days to take away my disgrace among the people."

...

THE BIRTH AND NAMING OF JOHN

57 Now the time had come for Elizabeth to give birth, and she had a son. 58 Then her neighbors and relatives heard that the Lord had shown her his great mercy, and they rejoiced with her.

59 When they came to circumcise the child on the eighth day, they were going to name him Zechariah, after his father. 60 But his mother responded, "No. He will be called John."

61 Then they said to her, "None of your relatives has that name." 62 So they motioned to his father to find out what he wanted him to be called. 63 He asked for a writing tablet and wrote, "His name is John." And they were all amazed. 64 Immediately his mouth was opened and his tongue set free, and he began to speak, praising God. 65 Fear came on all those who lived around them, and all these things were being talked about throughout the hill country of Judea. 66 All who heard about him took it to heart, saying, "What then will this child become?" For, indeed, the Lord's hand was with him.

EPHESIANS 2:4–5

4 But God, who is rich in mercy, because of his great love that he had for us, 5 made us alive with Christ even though we were dead in trespasses. You are saved by grace!

1 PETER 1:3–6

A LIVING HOPE

3 Blessed be the God and Father of our Lord Jesus Christ. Because of his great mercy he has given us new birth into a living hope through the resurrection of Jesus Christ from the dead 4 and into an inheritance that is imperishable, undefiled, and unfading, kept in heaven for you. 5 You are being guarded by God's power through faith for a salvation that is ready to be revealed in the last time. 6 You rejoice in this, even though now for a short time, if necessary, you suffer grief in various trials...

12.22.2020

WRITE A PRAYER BEGINNING WITH:

JESUS, YOU CAME TO BRING MERCY.

You came not to be a judge but to show us mercy and rescue us from judgment. How this plays out in real time is hard for me to understand, but I ask you to continue to provide me mercy, hope, peace, and understanding every morning. Jesus, I surrender to your mercy.

How have you seen God's mercy in your life? How can you extend this mercy to others?

God has shown me mercy be providing me a way out of my addiction and allowing me the opportunity to build a better, beautiful marriage. I must learn to extend mercy to Leslie in our marriage and put her needs above mine in all things.

THEN HER NEIGHBORS AND RELATIVES HEARD THAT THE LORD HAD SHOWN HER HIS GREAT MERCY, AND THEY REJOICED WITH HER.
LUKE 1:58

TO EXALT THE HUMBLE

LUKE 1:26–56

GABRIEL PREDICTS JESUS'S BIRTH

26 In the sixth month, the angel Gabriel was sent by God to a town in Galilee called Nazareth, 27 to a virgin engaged to a man named Joseph, of the house of David. The virgin's name was Mary. 28 And the angel came to her and said, "Greetings, favored woman! The Lord is with you." 29 But she was deeply troubled by this statement, wondering what kind of greeting this could be. 30 Then the angel told her, "Do not be afraid, Mary, for you have found favor with God. 31 Now listen: You will conceive and give birth to a son, and you will name him Jesus. 32 He will be great and will be called the Son of the Most High, and the Lord God will give him the throne of his father David. 33 He will reign over the house of Jacob forever, and his kingdom will have no end."

34 Mary asked the angel, "How can this be, since I have not had sexual relations with a man?"

35 The angel replied to her, "The Holy Spirit will come upon you, and the power of the Most High will overshadow you. Therefore, the holy one to be born will be called the Son of God. 36 And consider your relative Elizabeth—even she has conceived a son in her old age, and this is the sixth month for her who was called childless. 37 For nothing will be impossible with God."

38 "See, I am the Lord's servant," said Mary. "May it happen to me as you have said." Then the angel left her.

MARY'S VISIT TO ELIZABETH

39 In those days Mary set out and hurried to a town in the hill country of Judah 40 where she entered Zechariah's house and greeted Elizabeth. 41 When Elizabeth heard

Mary's greeting, the baby leaped inside her, and Elizabeth was filled with the Holy Spirit. [42] Then she exclaimed with a loud cry, "Blessed are you among women, and your child will be blessed! [43] How could this happen to me, that the mother of my Lord should come to me? [44] For you see, when the sound of your greeting reached my ears, the baby leaped for joy inside me. [45] Blessed is she who has believed that the Lord would fulfill what he has spoken to her!"

MARY'S PRAISE

[46] And Mary said:

My soul magnifies the Lord,
[47] and my spirit rejoices in God my Savior,
[48] because he has looked with favor
on the humble condition of his servant.
Surely, from now on all generations
will call me blessed,
[49] because the Mighty One
has done great things for me,
and his name is holy.
[50] His mercy is from generation
   to generation
on those who fear him.
[51] He has done a mighty deed with his arm;
he has scattered the proud
because of the thoughts of their hearts;
[52] he has toppled the mighty from
   their thrones
and exalted the lowly.
[53] He has satisfied the hungry with
   good things
and sent the rich away empty.
[54] He has helped his servant Israel,
remembering his mercy
[55] to Abraham and his descendants forever,
just as he spoke to our ancestors.

[56] And Mary stayed with her about three months; then she returned to her home.

JAMES 4:6-10

[6] But he gives greater grace. Therefore he says:

God resists the proud
but gives grace to the humble.

[7] Therefore, submit to God. Resist the devil, and he will flee from you. [8] Draw near to God, and he will draw near to you. Cleanse your hands, sinners, and purify your hearts, you double-minded. [9] Be miserable and mourn and weep. Let your laughter be turned to mourning and your joy to gloom. [10] Humble yourselves before the Lord, and he will exalt you.

12.23.2020

WRITE A PRAYER BEGINNING WITH:

JESUS,
YOU EXALT
THE HUMBLE.

Jesus exalts the humble, and He also humbled Himself. Use this space to reflect on Jesus's humility, not only in His life, but beginning with His birth.

You not only exalt and use and lift up those who are in a lowly humble state physically and financially, but You also exalt those who are spiritually humble. Lord, please help me to learn how to be spiritually & truly humble in my mind — I will work to learn humility, but I need your power and help.

Jesus showed ultimate humility and love by coming to earth. I think of it kind of like getting down on the floor and playing with my kids at their level and on their terms. In that moment, I give up some of my power and will and surrender to what they want to do. In those moments, I truly connect w/ them and Jesus connected with us by humbling himself and becoming human.

THEN THE ANGEL TOLD HER, "DO NOT BE AFRAID, MARY, FOR YOU HAVE FOUND FAVOR WITH GOD."
LUKE 1:30

CINNAMON ROLLS

DIFFICULTY LEVEL

PREP TIME

30 MINS

RISE TIME

1 HR 10 MINS

COOK TIME

25 MINS

SERVES

12

DOUGH

1 cup milk

1 packet active dry yeast

2 eggs, room temperature

⅓ cup salted butter, melted

1 teaspoon salt

½ cup sugar

4 ½ cups flour

CINNAMON SUGAR FILLING

10 tablespoons butter, softened

1 ¼ cups brown sugar, packed

3 tablespoons cinnamon

CHRISTMAS EVE

Heat milk to 115°F. Don't get it too hot or it will kill your yeast! Between 110°F and 120°F is ideal.

Add warm milk and yeast to bowl of stand mixer, stir, and let it sit for 5 minutes.

Mix in eggs, melted butter, salt, and sugar. Carefully add flour until just combined, then let sit for another 5 minutes.

Use the dough hook to knead the dough on medium for 5 minutes.

Lightly oil a large bowl, then place your dough in it and cover with a wet kitchen towel. Set bowl in a warm place to rise until the dough doubles in size, between 30 minutes to an hour.

While the dough is rising, make the filling. Cream together softened butter, brown sugar, cinnamon, and salt.

Once your dough has risen, place it on a floured work surface and roll it out to a large rectangle, about 2 feet by 1 foot.

Spread the filling over the rectangle of dough.

Tip: This is a great step for kids to help with!

Roll up the rectangle from the long edge into a tight cinnamon roll log. Cut the log into 12 equal pieces with a sharp knife, letting the knife do the work to avoid pushing out the filling or smooshing your layers together.

Grease a 9x13 baking pan and place the rolls in it side by side. Cover with plastic wrap and place in the refrigerator overnight.

FROSTING

½ to ¾ cup heavy cream
(for pouring over rolls)

8 ounces cream cheese, softened

½ cup butter, softened

2 cups powdered sugar

½ to 1 tablespoon vanilla extract

CHRISTMAS MORNING

Set out your cinnamon rolls, heavy cream, and cream cheese on the counter to warm up while the oven preheats. Your rolls should have risen slightly overnight.

Preheat oven to 375°F. Pour heavy cream over and around the cinnamon rolls in the pan.

Place the rolls in the oven and bake for 25 minutes, rotating halfway through, until the tops are slightly browned.

Set the rolls out to cool and prepare frosting by combining cream cheese, butter, powdered sugar, and vanilla extract with a mixer until well combined and creamy.

When the cinnamon rolls have cooled but are still warm, frost them.

Serve and enjoy!

CHRIST MAS

**TO
OFFER
US
HIS
PEACE**

EVE

Blessed are the peacemakers,
for they will be called sons of God.

LUKE 2:8-20, 25-40

THE SHEPHERDS AND THE ANGELS

[8] In the same region, shepherds were staying out in the fields and keeping watch at night over their flock. [9] Then an angel of the Lord stood before them, and the glory of the Lord shone around them, and they were terrified. [10] But the angel said to them, "Don't be afraid, for look, I proclaim to you good news of great joy that will be for all the people: [11] Today in the city of David a Savior was born for you, who is the Messiah, the Lord. [12] This will be the sign for you: You will find a baby wrapped tightly in cloth and lying in a manger."

[13] Suddenly there was a multitude of the heavenly host with the angel, praising God and saying:

> [14] Glory to God in the highest heaven,
> and peace on earth to people he favors!

[15] When the angels had left them and returned to heaven, the shepherds said to one another, "Let's go straight to Bethlehem and see what has happened, which the Lord has made known to us."

[16] They hurried off and found both Mary and Joseph, and the baby who was lying in the manger. [17] After seeing them, they reported the message they were told about this child, [18] and all who heard it were amazed at what the shepherds said to them. [19] But Mary was treasuring up all these things in her heart and meditating on them. [20] The shepherds returned, glorifying and praising God for all the things they had seen and heard, which were just as they had been told.

...

SIMEON'S PROPHETIC PRAISE

[25] There was a man in Jerusalem whose name was Simeon. This man was righteous and devout, looking forward to Israel's consolation, and the Holy Spirit was on him. [26] It had been revealed to him by the Holy Spirit

that he would not see death before he saw the Lord's Messiah. ²⁷ Guided by the Spirit, he entered the temple. When the parents brought in the child Jesus to perform for him what was customary under the law, ²⁸ Simeon took him up in his arms, praised God, and said,

²⁹ Now, Master,
you can dismiss your servant in peace,
as you promised.
³⁰ For my eyes have seen your salvation.
³¹ You have prepared it
in the presence of all peoples—
³² a light for revelation to the Gentiles
and glory to your people Israel.

³³ His father and mother were amazed at what was being said about him. ³⁴ Then Simeon blessed them and told his mother Mary, "Indeed, this child is destined to cause the fall and rise of many in Israel and to be a sign that will be opposed— ³⁵ and a sword will pierce your own soul—that the thoughts of many hearts may be revealed."

ANNA'S TESTIMONY

³⁶ There was also a prophetess, Anna, a daughter of Phanuel, of the tribe of Asher. She was well along in years, having lived with her husband seven years after her marriage, ³⁷ and was a widow for eighty-four years. She did not leave the temple, serving God night and day with fasting and prayers. ³⁸ At that very moment, she came up and began to thank God and to speak about him to all who were looking forward to the redemption of Jerusalem.

THE FAMILY'S RETURN TO NAZARETH

³⁹ When they had completed everything according to the law of the Lord, they returned to Galilee, to their own town of Nazareth. ⁴⁰ The boy grew up and became strong, filled with wisdom, and God's grace was on him.

LUKE 10:5-6

⁵ "Whatever house you enter, first say, 'Peace to this household.' ⁶ If a person of peace is there, your peace will rest on him; but if not, it will return to you."

JOHN 14:27

"Peace I leave with you. My peace I give to you. I do not give to you as the world gives. Don't let your heart be troubled or fearful."

12.24.2020

WRITE A PRAYER BEGINNING WITH:

JESUS, YOU OFFER US YOUR PEACE.

Think about the past week, month, and year. How has Jesus's birth brought peace to your own life?

Peace that was not just for the world & Israel at the time of your birth, but instead you offer peace for all time. You bring peace into our lives, my life, in the difficult times when I have no rest. You also promise peace on earth and deliverance from suffering. I believe you will keep your promises and provide peace!

Jesus's peace has been clear in my life recently as He has assured me that He is not done working in my life and marriage. I know that He requires me to do my part by working to draw closer to Him and learn about the obstacles to that that exist in my life. But I also know that He will honor that work by providing peace through the rough patches.

GLORY TO GOD IN THE HIGHEST HEAVEN, AND PEACE ON EARTH TO PEOPLE HE FAVORS!
LUKE 2:14

CHRIST MAS

DAY
27

**JESUS
CHRIST**
IS
BORN!

DAY

² In the last days
the mountain of the LORD's house will be established
at the top of the mountains
and will be raised above the hills.
All nations will stream to it,
³ and many peoples will come and say,
"Come, let's go up to the mountain of the LORD,
to the house of the God of Jacob.
He will teach us about his ways
so that we may walk in his paths."
For instruction will go out of Zion
and the word of the LORD from Jerusalem.

MATTHEW 2:1-12

WISE MEN VISIT THE KING

¹ After Jesus was born in Bethlehem of Judea in the days of King Herod, wise men from the east arrived in Jerusalem, ² saying, "Where is he who has been born king of the Jews? For we saw his star at its rising and have come to worship him."

³ When King Herod heard this, he was deeply disturbed, and all Jerusalem with him. ⁴ So he assembled all the chief priests and scribes of the people and asked them where the Messiah would be born.

⁵ "In Bethlehem of Judea," they told him, "because this is what was written by the prophet:

⁶ And you, Bethlehem, in the land of Judah,
are by no means least among the rulers of Judah:
Because out of you will come a ruler
who will shepherd my people Israel."

⁷ Then Herod secretly summoned the wise men and asked them the exact time the star appeared. ⁸ He sent them to Bethlehem and said, "Go and search carefully for the child. When you find him, report back to me so that I too can go and worship him."

⁹ After hearing the king, they went on their way. And there it was—the star they had seen at its rising. It led them until it came and stopped above the place where the child was.

¹⁰ When they saw the star, they were overwhelmed with joy.

¹¹ Entering the house, they saw the child with Mary his mother, and falling to their knees, they worshiped him. Then they opened their treasures and presented him with gifts: gold, frankincense, and myrrh. ¹² And being warned in a dream not to go back to Herod, they returned to their own country by another route.

EPHESIANS 4:4-6

⁴ There is one body and one Spirit—just as you were called to one hope at your calling— ⁵ one Lord, one faith, one baptism. ⁶ one God and Father of all, who is above all and through all and in all.

12.25.2020

WRITE A PRAYER BEGINNING WITH:

JESUS, THANK YOU FOR ALL YOU WERE BORN TO DO.

Thank you for coming to earth to be a living example of how to live out a life that is ~~worthy at~~ healthy and whole. Thank you for being the ultimate example of what ~~real~~ love and sacrifice looks like. Please help me to learn as much as I can about you so that I can follow your example for right living each day.

What about the birth of your Savior is most meaningful to you this year? Spend time rejoicing today in the wonder and blessing of Jesus's birth.

Jesus being born is the beginning of Him being willing to die for our sins. He was willing to do all it took to restore us to relationship with the Father. What a great picture of love and restoration!

FALLING TO THEIR KNEES, THEY WORSHIPED HIM.
MATTHEW 2:11

GOD REST YE MERRY, GENTLEMEN

TUNE
TRADITIONAL ENGLISH CAROL

1. God rest ye merr - y, gen tle - men, let no - thing you dis - may, Re -
2. In Beth - le - hem, in Is ra - el, this bless - èd Babe was born, And
3. From God our heaven - ly Fa - ther a bless - èd an - gel came; And
4. "Fear not, then," said the an - gel, "Let no - thing you a - fright This
5. The shep - herds at those tid - ings re - joic - ed much in mind, And
6. But when to Beth - le - hem they came where our dear Sav - ior lay, They
7. Now to the Lord sing prais - es all you with - in this place, And
8. God bless the ruler of this house, and send him long to reign, And

- mem - ber Christ our Sav - ior was born on Christ - mas Day; To
laid with - in a man - ger up - on this bless - èd morn; The
un - to cer - tain shep - herds brought tid - ings of the same; How
day is born a Sav - ior of a pure vir - gin bright, To
left their flocks a - feed - ing in tem - pest, storm and wind, And
found Him in a man - ger where ox - en feed on hay; His
with true love and brother - hood each o - ther now em - brace; This
many a mer - ry Christ - mas may live to see a - gain; A-

Refrain

save us all from Satan's power when we were gone a - stray.
which His mo - ther Mar - y did no - thing take in scorn.
that in Beth - le - hem was born the Son of God by name.
free all those who trust in Him from Sa - tan's power and might." O tid - ings of
went to Beth - l'em straighta - way this bless - èd Babe to find.
mo - ther Ma - ry kneel - ing un - to the Lord did pray.
ho - ly tide of Christ - mas all o - thers doth de - face.
- mong your friends and kin - dred that live both far and near.

com - fort and joy, com - fort and joy; O tid - ings of com - fort and joy.

DAY
28

GRACE DAY

AS THIS SEASON OF ANTICIPATION CLOSES, WE CONTINUE TO REJOICE AT THE MIRACLE OF CHRIST'S COMING AND LONG FOR OUR SAVIOR'S PROMISED RETURN.

On this day after Christmas, spend time reflecting on all that Jesus has done, is doing, and will do.

BUT MARY WAS TREASURING UP ALL THESE THINGS IN HER HEART AND MEDITATING ON THEM.

LUKE 2:19

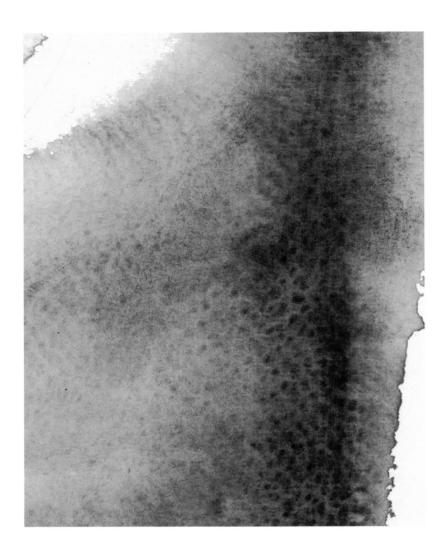

REJOICE

THE FIRST SUNDAY OF CHRISTMASTIDE

On this first Sunday after Christmas, we celebrate that Jesus Christ is born! He brings hope, peace, joy, and love to all who turn to Him, both in this life and in the eternal life to come. Spend this week memorizing or meditating on John 1:14 as you rejoice in the advent of our Savior.

THE WORD BECAME
FLESH AND DWELT
AMONG US. WE
OBSERVED HIS GLORY,
THE GLORY AS THE ONE
AND ONLY SON FROM
THE FATHER, FULL OF
GRACE AND TRUTH.

JOHN 1:14

WHERE DID I SPEND CHRISTMAS DAY?

2501 Giant Oaks Dr.
Pittsburgh. (USC)

WHAT TIME DID I WAKE UP?

6:20 AM

PM

WHAT WAS THE WEATHER LIKE?
(CIRCLE ONE)

HIGH

LOW

WHO DID I CELEBRATE CHRISTMAS WITH?

My family!
Leslie, Eli,
Brooks, Violet,
Jade, Baby #5

WHAT MADE US LAUGH?

WHAT TRADITION MEANT THE MOST TO ME THIS YEAR?

The advent
devotional w/
the kids.

WHAT WAS MY FAVORITE CHRISTMAS SONG THIS YEAR?

TITLE

ARTIST

I LOVED
GIVING

GIFT She Reads Truth Bible

TO Leslie

I LOVED
RECEIVING

GIFT Apple Watch

FROM Leslie.

MY FAVORITE
ADVENT SCRIPTURE FROM THIS STUDY

HOW DID I SEE GOD
AT WORK IN 2020?

WHAT HAS GOD TAUGHT ME
ABOUT HIS CHARACTER?

WHAT HAS GOD TAUGHT
ME ABOUT MYSELF?

MY FAVORITE
HE READS TRUTH STUDY

WHAT WAS AN
UNEXPECTED
JOY THIS PAST
YEAR?

WHAT WAS AN
UNEXPECTED
SORROW?

THIS YEAR, I'M GRATEFUL FOR

THIS YEAR, I'M MOST PROUD OF

THE
MOST CHALLENGING
PART OF MY YEAR

THE
HIGHLIGHT
OF MY YEAR

MY
PRAYER FOR
2021

DOWNLOAD THE APP

VISIT
hereadstruth.com

SHOP
shophereadstruth.com

CONTACT
hello@hereadstruth.com

CONNECT
#HeReadsTruth

LISTEN
She Reads Truth Podcast

CSB BOOK ABBREVIATIONS

OLD TESTAMENT
Genesis – Gn
Exodus – Ex
Leviticus – Lv
Numbers – Nm
Deuteronomy – Dt
Joshua – Jos
Judges – Jdg
Ruth – Ru
1 Samuel – 1Sm
2 Samuel – 2Sm
1 Kings – 1Kg
2 Kings – 2Kg
1 Chronicles – 1Ch
2 Chronicles – 2Ch
Ezra – Ezr
Nehemiah – Neh
Esther – Est
Job – Jb
Psalms – Ps
Proverbs – Pr
Ecclesiastes – Ec
Song of Solomon – Sg

Isaiah – Is
Jeremiah – Jr
Lamentations – Lm
Ezekiel – Ezk
Daniel – Dn
Hosea – Hs
Joel – Jl
Amos – Am
Obadiah – Ob
Jonah – Jnh
Micah – Mc
Nahum – Nah
Habakkuk – Hab
Zephaniah – Zph
Haggai – Hg
Zechariah – Zch
Malachi – Mal

NEW TESTAMENT
Matthew – Mt
Mark – Mk
Luke – Lk
John – Jn

Acts – Ac
Romans – Rm
1 Corinthians – 1Co
2 Corinthians – 2Co
Galatians – Gl
Ephesians – Eph
Philippians – Php
Colossians – Col
1 Thessalonians – 1Th
2 Thessalonians – 2Th
1 Timothy – 1Tm
2 Timothy – 2Tm
Titus – Ti
Philemon – Phm
Hebrews – Heb
James – Jms
1 Peter – 1Pt
2 Peter – 2Pt
1 John – 1Jn
2 John – 2Jn
3 John – 3Jn
Jude – Jd
Revelation – Rv

HE READS TRUTH | BIBLE

The *He Reads Truth Bible* includes a robust selection of thoughtfully crafted theological extras to draw the reader back to Scripture and foster a growing affection for God and His Word.

Featuring the Christian Standard Bible (CSB) text, the *He Reads Truth Bible* maintains accuracy without sacrificing readability, making it easier to engage with Scripture's life-changing message and share it with others.

**USE CODE HRTB15 FOR 15% OFF
YOUR NEW HE READS TRUTH BIBLE**

SHOPHEREADSTRUTH.COM

READY
FOR YOUR
NEXT STEP?

At He Reads Truth, we have one simple mission: Men in the Word of God every day. To support this mission, we offer a variety of resources and tools to enhance your time in God's Word.

HE READS TRUTH APP

The He Reads Truth app is a functional and accessible Bible-reading tool created to help men around the world connect with God's Word and each other, any time and anywhere.

Within the app, you'll find helpful resources like devotionals or interactive questions to help you further engage with each Bible reading plan. You can also read the Bible, participate in community discussions, and download lockscreens for Scripture memorization.

Download on the App Store or Google Play.

HEREADSTRUTH.COM

All of our reading plans and devotionals are available at HeReadsTruth.com. This is an easy, convenient way to invite your family, friends, and coworkers to read God's Word with you.